THE TRANSPARENT TAROT
Emily Carding

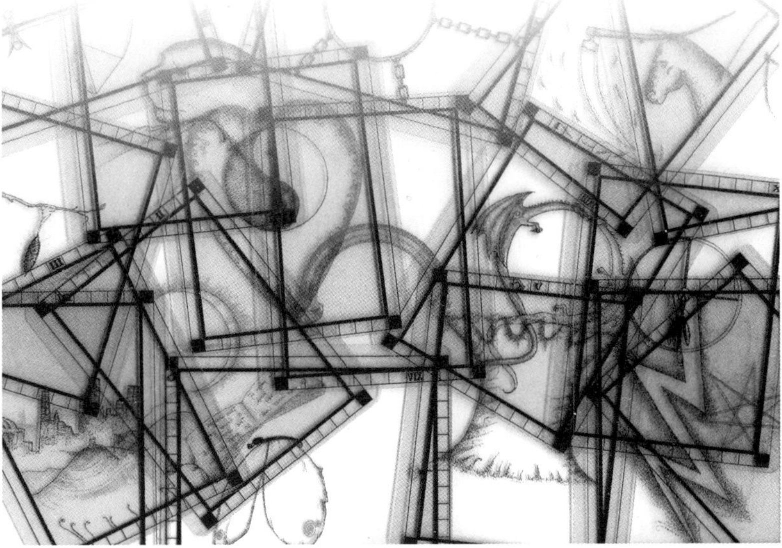

Schiffer Publishing Ltd

4880 Lower Valley Road, Atglen, Pa 19310

Published by Schiffer Publishing, Ltd.
4880 Lower Valley Road
Atglen, PA 19310
Phone: (610) 593-1777; Fax: (610) 593-2002
E-mail: Info@schifferbooks.com

For our complete selection of fine books on this and related subjects, please visit our website at www.schifferbooks.com. You may also write for a free catalog.

This book may be purchased from the publisher. Please try your bookstore first.

We are always looking for people to write books on new and related subjects. If you have an idea for a book, please contact us at proposals@schifferbooks.com.

Schiffer Publishing's titles are available at special discounts for bulk purchases for sales promotions or premiums. Special editions, including personalized covers, corporate imprints, and excerpts can be created in large quantities for special needs. For more information, contact the publisher.

Designed by RoS
Type set in Brisk/NewBskvll BT

ISBN: 978-0-7643-3003-2
Printed in China

DEDICATION

To all those who walk with me,
in this world and in spirit.

ACKNOWLEDGEMENTS

There are many, many people I wish to thank. Firstly, I give my thanks to the universe, the God and Goddess and my guides for the inspiration for this deck, and for giving me Jules, the most wonderful, magickal and supportive Pooky Bear in the world. And thank you to Jules, for being that bear.

Thank you to Willow, for putting up with a grumpy, busy Mummy.

Huge thanks must go to Dinah, my editor, for her incredible enthusiasm and wonderful work. Without her, this deck may never have been produced.

A big thank you to Naomi for taking the time to write a super foreword!

Thank you to Adam McLean for all the help and many creative efforts.

Thank you also to John and Caitlín Matthews for being wonderful teachers and inspirations, and for lots of encouragement when the project was in its early stages.

Big thanks to Sophie Nusslé for taking time to read through my musings and for great advice and comments.

Thanks to Michael Hurst, for the history lesson, and to Baba Prague, JMD, Gayla, and Le Pendu from Aeclectic for pointing me in the right direction.

And huge thanks to all my other friends on the Aeclectic Tarot forum, who have been an endless source of strength, support and humor! I wonder if Gregory really will be the first to get her copy...

FOREWORD

Having found inspiration in the images of the Tarot for many years, I am delighted by Emily Carding's sheer originality and new vision, *The Transparent Tarot*. In an area constrained by tradition, innovation is unexpected, but Emily's concept has achieved a remarkable feat. *The Transparent Tarot* pays due homage to tradition while taking the familiar images into a new realm. The traditional pack of cards has become a series of transparencies, the characters of the Major Arcana now appear in their essential forms, simple and minimal, and the Minor Arcana appear as silhouetted figures. The result is a new fusion between a modern material and the realm of archetypal ideas. Overlapping transparencies enable the reader to combine several cards and interpret symbols like layers in the mind. Emily's considerable design and graphic skill enables each of the cards to interrelate visually with others; the symbolic connections then speak for themselves.

Emily Carding is emerging as one of our most original and talented Tarot artists, this landmark deck forms a nodal point on the Tarot family tree permitting a new course of development to unfold. Whether you are a collector of outstanding Tarot design, a reader, or a student of Tarot, *The Transparent Tarot* will engage your full attention just as it did for me.

—Naomi Ozaniec, October 2007

INTRODUCTION

Welcome to your guide to *The Transparent Tarot*. This is written not as a definitive book of instructions, nor as a set of outlines within which you must work, but as a foundation for you to launch into your own exploration of Tarot. As such, before you begin this book in earnest, I will strongly suggest one thing: Put it down.

Now, pick up the cards and look through them, play with them, whatever you feel drawn to do—except possibly spread them too wide over a patterned carpet, as you'll probably lose a few that way. They *are* transparent, after all! Using a bright white background (or the provided white reading cloth), spread out the cards and try forming a few pictures. Without referring to the book, start forming your own impression of the cards, their feeling and meanings. Perhaps you could try using them to form an image that you feel reflects your current personality or situation, or just create images that you think are pretty. Whatever you decide to do, the important thing is that you build up your own relationship with the cards early on, before you read my own theories and ideas about what they mean and how you could use them. You may wish to keep the cards handy as you read through the book, so you can see the full color detail of the images.

Something I will repeat and emphasize in this book is that this deck of cards is now *yours*. It is your *tool*, and so it is for you, not I, to decide how it will be used and what various things may or may not mean. *The Transparent Tarot* is a tool for unlocking your intuition, and as such anything I have to say as its designer is simply based on my personal research and understanding of the cards. It is not meant to dictate anything to you. In fact, you may find your own completely unrelated meanings for the images on the cards, and that is great! The information in this book is simply there to support you in your quest for your own understanding, provide you with some fresh angles you might not have thought of before, and hopefully give you the confidence and inspiration necessary to find profound benefit from the cards.

CONTENTS

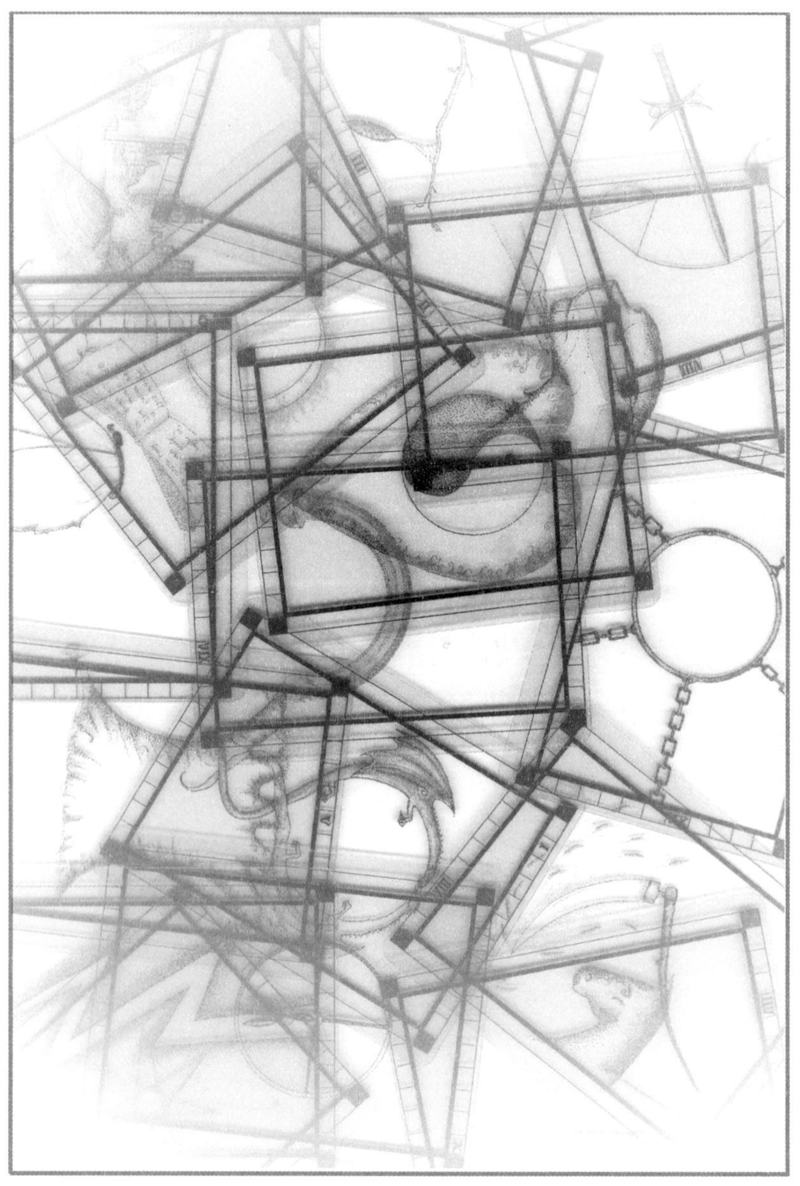

Chapter One
WHAT IS TAROT?

A Tarot deck usually consists of seventy-eight cards with a very specific structure, consisting of twenty-two cards known as the Major Arcana, and fifty-six cards known as the Minor Arcana. The cards of the Major Arcana represent major archetypal forces in our lives, and the Minor Arcana, which stand for everyday events, have many similarities with a pack of playing cards, consisting of court cards, Aces and numbered pips, or small cards.

This structure may seem unimportant or unremarkable to a beginner, but those who have scratched even the surface of esoteric lore have noted that this structure coincides with the ancient Hebrew teachings of the Qabalah and the Tree of Life, as well as numerology and various other correspondences which have appeared over time. This has lead to many Tarot enthusiasts through the ages to debate over the mystical origins of the cards and their images, particularly the twenty-two cards of the Major Arcana, which are rich in ancient symbolism. Some believe their origins can be attributed to Ancient Egypt, or even the lost land of Atlantis, the sacred images being used to conceal and pass down ancient magickal knowledge. Others prefer to stick to the historical origins for which there is concrete physical evidence. Personally, I believe that whatever the earthly origins of Tarot may be, they are a gift to us which can aid us in our search for self-knowledge, understanding, and universal truth. And though it is interesting and rewarding to study the roots of where Tarot has come from and where and what it has been, with *The Transparent Tarot* I am far more interested in looking at where Tarot is *going*.

The Evolution of Tarot

Although there may be some disagreement as to the true meaning and origins of Tarot, one thing that we can all be sure of is that Tarot is evolving. If we look very briefly at the recorded history of the cards, they first emerged in their current structure in fifteenth century Italy. This is when the twenty-two 'trionfi', as the trumps of the Major Arcana were then called, were first joined with traditional playing cards, which had been around in Europe for about a century beforehand. Also called 'Tarocchi', for the next two hundred years the cards kept their standard imagery, the small cards being nothing but elaborate pips at this point. The cards have always had imaginative uses. It is widely thought they were used for divination parlor games, a poetry game called 'Tarocchi appropriati', as well as playing the game of Tarot, which was popular at the time. This style of deck has become known as 'Tarot de Marseilles' and is still extremely popular with many readers and collectors.

Although some variations, such as the Minchiate deck were created, and interest in using the cards for divination and occult use started to gain popularity in the eighteenth and nineteenth centuries, the cards themselves did not change greatly until the creation of what is now known as the Rider-Waite Tarot. This was conceived in the early twentieth century by the occultist and mystic Arthur Edward Waite and the artist Pamela Colman-Smith, and was the first deck to include fully illustrated scenes for the pip cards. Waite used the cards as a vehicle by which to communicate mystical concepts of the evolution of the soul. He used symbols in order to directly communicate with the subconscious and higher self, and created meaningful scenes for the Minor Arcana in order to aid the intuition of those using the cards.

Since this evolutionary leap was taken, Tarot has been used

as a vehicle for many to either explore their personal ideology or to share it with others. Another notable example of this is the creation of the infamous Aleister Crowley and artist Lady Frieda Harris, the Thoth Tarot, which is a complex and absorbing system in itself and has spawned many clones.

Since these landmark decks, literally thousands have been created. Some are profoundly spiritual, some downright silly, yet they all have their place. There are so many different decks available now, that any individual should be able to find one that suits them perfectly. Tarot now has many uses, beyond the original game and divination. It is a tool which can be used for meditation, pathworking, magick, brainstorming, and even therapy. There are now even digital decks which can be viewed and used online. Yet until now, Tarot has existed as a set of two dimensional images, which only the imagination could mingle and combine. *The Transparent Tarot* is the first deck which offers the ability to truly combine the images, opening up almost infinite possibilities for interpretation and use, taking us into the future of Tarot with another bold step of evolution.

What Makes *The Transparent Tarot* Special?

The Transparent Tarot is a deck of simplified yet beautiful images which are designed to be able to be read in layers. The images are printed on transparent plastic so that when they are placed on a white background, they can be combined to create evocative scenes and pictures containing up to three or four cards each. This physical mingling of the cards has never before been conceived or attempted, literally adding a whole new dimension to Tarot and a myriad of new possibilities. The images themselves have been conceptualized in as simple yet profound a way as possible, in order to capture the essence of the universal meaning. The uncomplicated graphic design and absence of elaborate detail not only enables any card to combine with any other in the deck without excessive confusion, but also opens them up to wider possibilities of interpretation. *The Transparent Tarot* is a window into your own intuition, a gateway through which you can access your inner knowledge and your higher self.

It's also an awful lot of fun!

For beginners, this deck offers a way to learn the cards that is not only innovative, but organic and intuitive. It doesn't burden you with heaps of deeply significant or outdated symbolism, but gives you a tool which you can pick up and use with no prior knowledge or experience. Something that confounds many Tarot users early on is the difficulty in seeing how the cards affect each other in a reading—now this can be explored easily and directly by combining them into one image. The nature of this deck encourages experimentation and discovery, which is a great way to learn!

For more advanced students, or even experts, *The Transparent Tarot* offers a completely fresh perspective and ways of using the cards which have *never before been possible*. No matter how much you know or understand about Tarot and its various uses, this deck has something new to offer. Not only is it highly effective and entertaining to use for readings and divination, but it offers new ways to use the cards in magick, meditation, and creative brainstorming amongst the many possibilities. This Tarot is designed to engage that most useful of tools, the imagination, which can be effective in as simple a way as just playing with cards and seeing what arises. You may discover other applications for the cards while you work and play with them. So long as you treat the cards with respect, they will serve you well, however you wish to use them.

Caring for your cards

When not using your cards, it is best to keep them stored flat and wrapped in their cloth. You may also wish to keep them in an appropriate Tarot bag or box. If you wish to use a cloth other than the reading cloth provided with the deck, then silk is often favored, not only for its softness, but for its qualities as a natural psychic insulator. Many people choose to use certain crystals with their decks, to empower and protect them. You may simply choose to keep them in the box they came in, which is fine. The important thing is not to leave them lying around when you're not using them, as they may get lost, damaged, or acquired by sticky fingers! The nature of these cards means that you will need a plain white surface to read them on, and whilst paper or plastic will do, it would be a good idea to use the white cloth for readings. Those who use the cards a lot may even wish to invest in a light box, which are available from some art and craft stores, and will really illuminate your cards! This might be particularly nice for those who wish to use them in meditation.

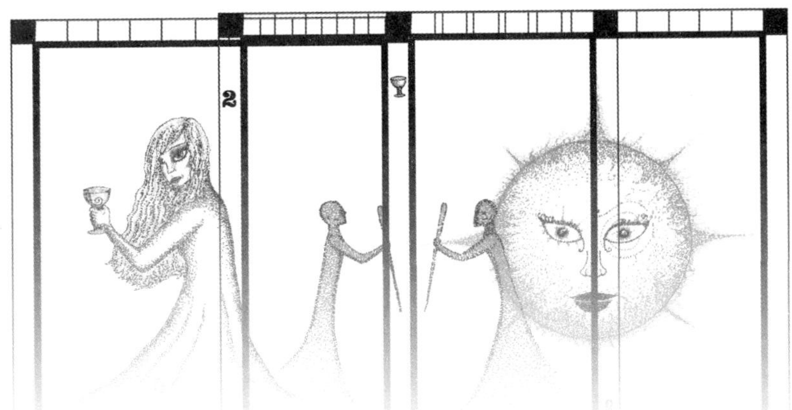

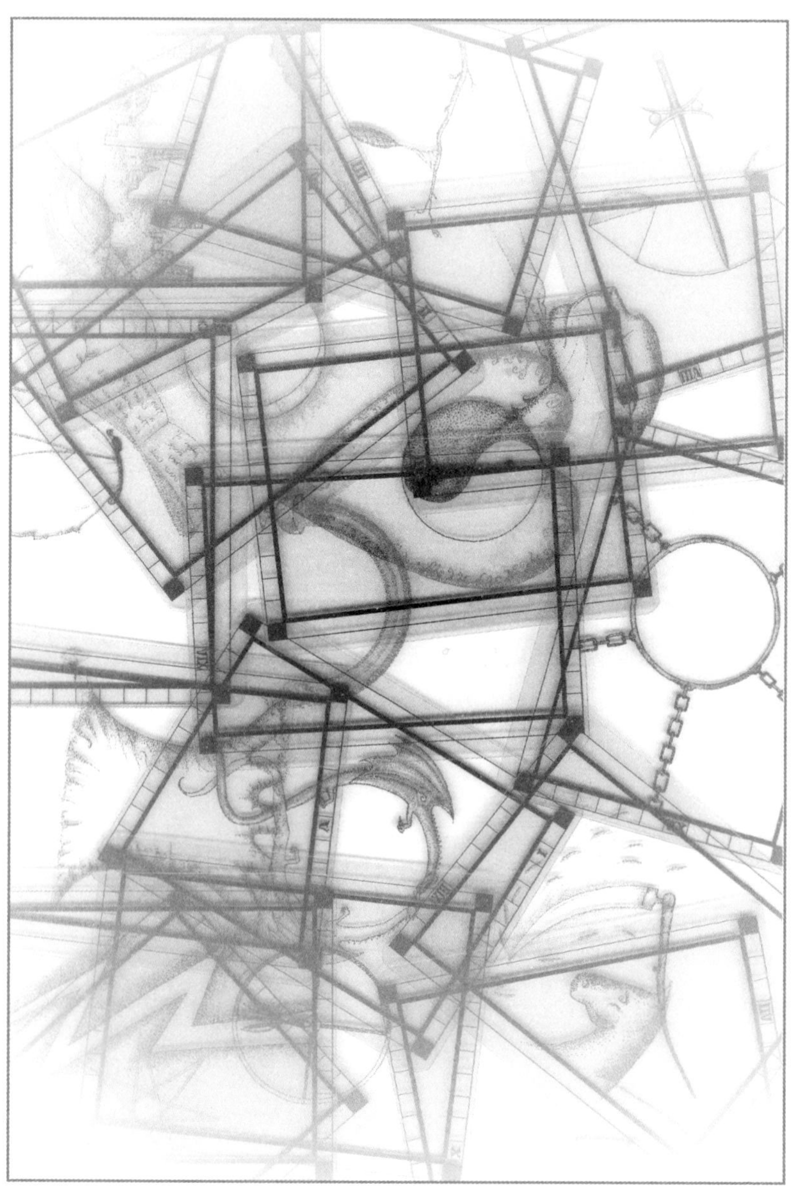

Chapter Two
CARD MEANINGS

Before we look at some suggested methods for using the cards, let's look at the meanings of the cards themselves. Again, I must emphasize that these meanings are only scratching the surface of what you will be able to discover yourself through using the cards. I have compiled traditional meanings as well as my own personal insights and interpretation in order to give you a solid base to work from. Generally, I have described the meaning in terms of the querent, which is the person asking the question, whether it is you or another party for whom you are reading.

When you are using the cards in a reading, they may in fact take on almost any meaning, as there are a myriad of contexts and variables involved. The intuition must be the final judge, as there is no limit to the effect that variance in question and personal circumstance can generate. I have however done my best to give as many suggestions for different dimensions to the cards as seemed reasonable, and have also included some examples to show how the cards may affect each other when combined.

Remember, this is *your* tool, for *your* work—enjoy!

THE MAJOR ARCANA

The twenty-two cards of the Major Arcana represent the great archetypes and universal forces that are at work in our lives. In traditional Tarot, these cards contain deeply significant and complex symbolism, usually surrounding a figure or figures intended to portray anthropomorphic versions of these abstract concepts. Because such images are already highly complex and involved in and of themselves, if they were to be combined in layers, they would not produce anything remotely resembling a coherent and readable image. For *The Transparent Tarot*, I have conceptualised each card of the Major Arcana as a single simple but powerful symbol. Sometimes these symbols have been derived from details which appear within traditional Tarot, whilst at other times it was more appropriate to devise an original symbol to encapsulate the meaning. Whilst the meaning of the cards is still consistent with traditional Tarot, the simplified form not only means that it should be possible to combine any of the cards together and form a meaningful image, but also that there is much more left to individual interpretation and intuition. These images speak directly to the subconscious, without involving the conscious mind in the process of unravelling and translating complex imagery. It also means there can be no confusion between the Major Arcana and the Minor Arcana. These distilled and de-personified archetypes act as the landscapes on which our everyday lives, as shown by the simple figures of the Minor Arcana, take place.

In the following section you will learn not only about the independent meanings of the cards, but how to interpret combined images, and how we can study connections between certain of the cards by combining them into one image.

As we explore the meanings of the Major Arcana, you will notice that these cards seem to tell a story of a great journey. This is sometimes called 'The Fool's Journey', as the first card of the Major Arcana, "The Fool", is popularly known as the hero of this quest. It is a journey from total innocence, through many challenges, triumphs, and insights, to enlightenment and wisdom. Although we may not realise it, these archetypes are all around us, constantly at work in our lives. They manifest as major stages and turning points in our lives, in influential figures, and in aspects of our own personalities. When you see a lot of cards from the Major Arcana appearing in your readings, it is a sign that current events are of great significance not only on an earthly level, but on a spiritual level. This is reflected on an aesthetic level within a reading, for any of the cards of the Major Arcana bring an extra dimension of beauty and colour to a combined image. If you can learn to use these cards in order to tune into these forces, you will not only be better prepared for what may be to come, but you will be able to see the greater lesson at work. Each one of us is the innocent 'Fool' on our own journey. If we can see each challenge and setback as an adventure or a valuable lesson, we will find our own path to wisdom. The cards of the Major Arcana can act as initiators, challengers, guides, and companions on our journey, enriching our lives and ensuring that we are not in for a dull ride!

As you use the deck and familiarize yourself with the cards, it is useful to make notes on your own observations about the Major Arcana, exploring such questions as:

How does the energy of this card affect a reading?

What cards seem to combine particularly well with this card?

Which cards work less well together? Why? What could this mean?

What do I think of when I see this card?

How does this card make me feel?

What smells/tastes/sounds do I associate with this card?

If this card could speak, what would it say?

Looking into these questions will help you to deepen your understanding of the cards, and improve your skills as a reader.

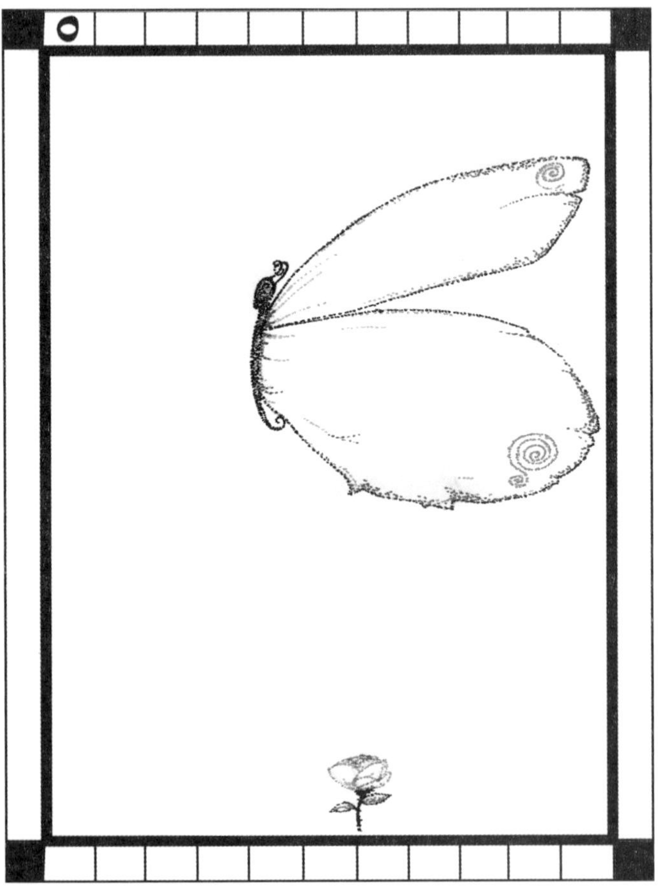

O-The Fool

Here we are at the beginning of the journey of life—the journey through the Major Arcana of the Tarot. The Fool is numbered 'zero', which in a sense makes him numberless. So what does this mean? The zero tells us that our journey starts in a void, in the very centre of our selves. The Fool is the inner spark of breath, soul, and action that must ignite before any true adventure can begin.

A popular portrayal of the Fool in many decks is that of a young figure walking carelessly towards the edge of a cliff, his belongings carried in a tiny pack on the end of his staff. There is usually a small dog or other animal biting at his ankle, and a white rose in his hand. In some decks you may also spot a butterfly.

In my quest to find the simplest image to sum up the Fool, I eventually settled on one of the smallest details from traditional Tarot, the white rose, in combination with a universally recognizable symbol, the butterfly. The white rose is readily accessible as a symbol of purity, but why the butterfly as the main feature? The butterfly and its incredible journey from caterpillar to chrysalis to winged beauty is a powerful symbol of transformation, and it is that potential for transformation that the Fool represents. Its flying form is also suggestive of the great 'leap of faith' that must be taken in order for this transformation to begin, for one thing is certain if you make such a leap—for better or worse, things will never be the same again. The subtle spirals on the butterfly's wings are an echo of the World card, the last card of the Major Arcana and the true potential contained within each of us.

Divinatory meaning

When the Fool appears in a reading, he almost always represents the querent or an aspect of themselves. The Fool is the great innocent, the one who is not afraid to ask the 'silly' question. But remember, without asking questions, how do we ever learn? It is, of all the cards, the Fool who has the most potential to become truly wise, as he approaches life with an open heart and mind, and sees the world with the eyes of a child. Within a combination, the Fool brings a sense of freedom and faith to a situation. If the other cards speak of a choice to be made, the Fool, so long as he is upright, will advise us to take the leap and trust that we have the wings to carry us safely. There is a certain quality of 'blessedness' about the Fool, which hints towards greater forces protecting us in what may seem to be risky actions.

However if the Fool appears reversed in your reading it is advisable to tread more carefully, and take a good look at where you are going before you make a move. Take your time with any decision, because the Fool reversed can often be a fool indeed.

Here is an example of a three-card combination featuring the Fool:

In this image, the Fool is combined with the Eight of Cups and the Ten of Wands. We can see the oppressed figure of the Ten of Wands at the bottom of the image, struggling with her burden. Directly above her we see her dream of leaving this weight behind and breaking free to a better future, as the figure of the Eight of Cups stretches his hand towards a 'Holy Grail'. There are still perhaps obstacles in the way.

After all, the burden is still carried, and there are still stairs to ascend before the goal is reached. But the presence of the Fool here shows us the true underlying nature of the querent that has been suppressed, and is longing to surface again. He speaks of the need to fly free, and offers protection and blessing for the needed change in life pattern. Fling aside those burdensome wands, and reach for your dreams.

The Fool is, in a sense, the hero of the Tarot story, and so is intended to combine equally favorably with any of the Major Arcana.

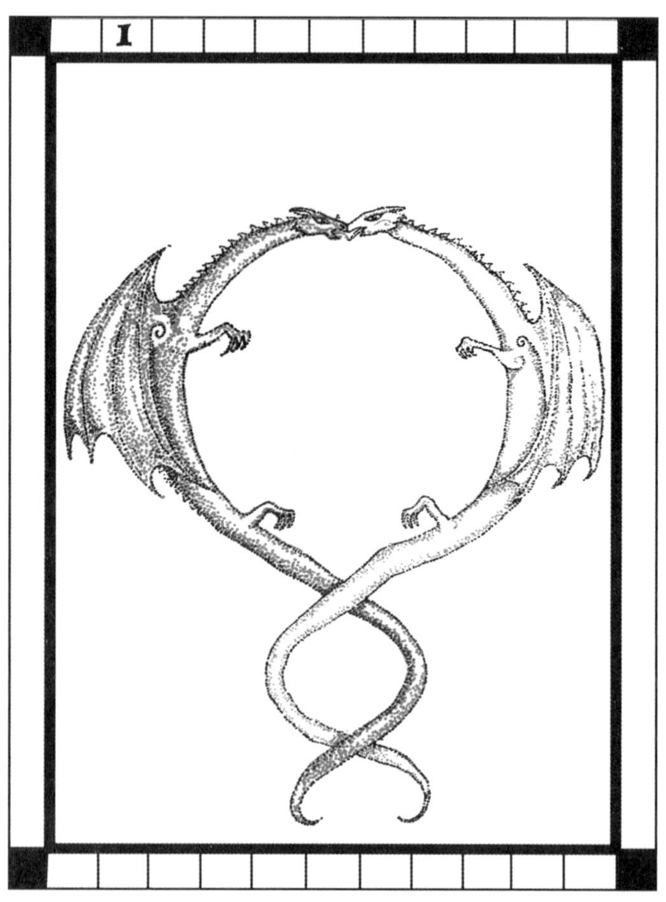

I-The Magician

To those who are familiar with Rider-Waite based imagery in the Tarot, this image of red and white dragons intertwining may seem very different from the Magician we are used to seeing—a male figure standing confidently in front of an altar on which the tools of his craft, a wand, cup, sword, and pentacle, (the four suits of the Tarot's Minor Arcana), are displayed. However, there are roots for my choice of symbol within established Tarot imagery. The robes the traditional Magician wears are colored red and white, as are the flowers surrounding him on the Rider-Waite card. The infinity symbol created by the dragons as they weave around each other is a symbol strongly associated with the Magician, normally appearing over his head. Those familiar with Aleister Crowley's Thoth Tarot may draw parallels between the dragons on this card and the serpents which weave around the staff of the Thoth's Magus. Also he is portrayed in some decks as wearing a serpent belt, its tail in its mouth, a symbol of occult knowledge and the infinite nature of the cosmos.

The serpent or dragon has been associated with magick and magicians throughout the ages. The red and white dragons specifically relate to one of the most well known, if not *the* most well known magician in world of mythology, Merlin. As a child, his vision of the two dragons battling in an underworld cave earned him a reputation as a seer, and saved him from being sacrificed by druids.

But what do the colors red and white represent? Throughout mythology and within Tarot itself we can see many interpretations for these colors, be it the blood of the mother's womb and seed of the father, the sun and moon, or the ancient Nordic myth of Fire and Ice, essentially what they encapsulate are the ingredients necessary for creation. Through this image, the four elements at the disposal of the Magician normally represented by his tools are distilled down to two polarized universal forces which contain the potential for the creation of the world. The Magician is the active, masculine aspect of creation. He is the will that brings thought into being.

Divinatory Meaning

Provided that the Magician appears to be representing the querent, he shows us that we have all we need to complete a task ahead. The Magician has the ability to bring will into form, and has all the elements at his disposal. When the Magician has his sights set on success, very little is going to stand in his way. On an obvious level, this card can of course refer to a magickal path, but on a more subtle level, he has the qualities of intelligence, passion, and determination that mean he generally gets his own way. The Magician is also associated with Mercury, which gives him the skills of communication and clarity of focus. If the Magician appears to represent a figure in the querent's life, he will be a highly charismatic and persuasive character of high intelligence and excellent communication skills.

If you should find the Magician ill-aspected in your reading, beware of tricksters and those who use their skills and superior abilities to manipulate others. Look closely at yourself, and ask if this could in fact be you who are guilty of this. When he is favorably aspected within a combination, he brings a sense that anything is possible, and that all aims can be achieved. Everything that is needed to see a task through to its conclusion is readily to hand—it is already within you.

Here is an example of a three-card combination featuring the Magician:

Here we see the Magician combined with the Queen of Swords and the Ace of Pentacles. The Queen of Swords may represent the querent or someone in a position of influence in their life. Her determination, intelligence, and independence are complemented by the skills of the Magician, and it seems unlikely that anything would stand in her way. The Magician appears to be framing the Ace of Pentacles. Perhaps this is the treasured goal that the Queen seeks. If so, it seems that it is within her grasp, if she can realize the potential of the Magician within her. Also noteworthy is that her eyes appeared obscured by the red dragon—perhaps she is blinded to the needs of others, by her lust for power? There is an air of inapproachability about the Queen which suggests that although she may achieve her goal of material security and success, the price might be an increased isolation. Since she is of a character that is often alone and self-sufficient, again aided by the Magician's talents and self-awareness, this may not be an unhappy loneliness, but rather a compromise that she is all too willing to make. The Magician's clear effect on this image is to put the querent's goal firmly in her hands, showing that she has all the resources needed to achieve her will.

The Magician is designed to combine particularly well with the High Priestess, as the two are paired as male and female polarities of Magick.

II
In the pages of
a secret book,
lies the key
to your inner Look
This insight is
a truer gaze,
The wisest light
to guide your days

II-The High Priestess

The symbols I have used for the High Priestess can be readily found on most traditional renderings of this card. Usually she is portrayed as a young, mysteriously beautiful, robed and veiled woman, sitting between two columns, one black, one white and with a book or scroll on her lap. She is crowned by a crescent or triple moon, with a crescent moon also often at her feet.

The crescent moon is of a deep and multi-layered significance. Within pagan tradition, it is related to the maiden aspect of the Goddess, and her beguiling purity. There is of course also the fact that the crescent moon speaks of promise of what is to come, the potential of a new journey to greater fulfillment and wisdom as she waxes to full. The light of the crescent moon is bright, cutting through the surrounding night sky like a saber, but it is most significant that despite the light it gives, most of the moon remains shrouded in darkness. So it is with the wisdom and guidance offered by the High Priestess. We can catch but a glimpse of her book under the crescent moon's silvery glow, as she holds many secrets behind the veil of night. As the simple rhyme on the book in this card hints, the key is to look within for the answers. The High Priestess is the female counterpart of the Magician, the receptive rather than active principle. The light of intuition that surfaces to guide us comes from a deep well of inner understanding, just as the crescent which shines its reflected light is only a tiny part of the whole moon. Without the unseen that lies in the shadows, the magickal sliver of light could not exist. She offers us but a glimpse of what lies behind the veil, but it is enough of a gift to know that the veil is there and that there is more beyond it to be discovered.

Divinatory Meaning

The High Priestess brings a quality of mystery to any reading in which she appears. Whereas the Magician surges forward into the world creating reality by his will, the High Priestess sits apart from the outer world and explores the realm within. She is the initiator into the greater mysteries and the keeper of the door into other worlds. Her calm and centered presence silently speaks of the strength of intuition and empowerment of the more traditionally female qualities, whether it be within a man or woman. As the light of the crescent gives away the existence of the darker whole, so the High Priestess can lead us to secret knowledge which remains unseen to others. She is the link, the bridge, between this world and the divine, and so, of all the cards, has the most to teach us about divination and the Tarot itself. If she appears to represent the querent within a reading, then it is time for that person to come into their own power, access their inner knowledge and start on a new path or level of self discovery. This may mean time alone in study and meditation, or it may mean facilitating such development for others. She may also appear in a reading to represent a teacher or initiator coming into the querent's life, from whom will be learnt powerful and strange lessons.

If the High Priestess should appear reversed, it may mean that the flow of intuition is blocked for some reason, or that strong feelings and knowledge from within are being repressed. False predictions may be made, or a teacher of the mysteries may not be all that she or he seems. Sometimes it is difficult to trust our own feelings and intuition, becoming difficult to tell what is real and what is fabricated, and signals become confused. Take the time to look deep within and try to block out the noise of the outer world. Your true intuition is there waiting still.

Within a combined image, the High Priestess brings a sense of calm and stillness, but also a sense of knowledge that remains hidden. Time must be taken to look deep within in order to see the truth of the situation which is unfolding. It is also possible that she speaks of a teacher who will be present to help you gain the needed knowledge.

Here is an example of a three-card combination featuring the High Priestess:

In this image, the Two of Swords appears to be the key figure, sitting within the book of the High Priestess, as the Three of Wands appears almost like a vision in the moon. This combination seems to speak strongly about initiation and coming into power through self knowledge. The Two of Swords sits confidently and calmly within the book of knowledge, taking the time to choose the direction his life will take. Through inner knowledge, the path ahead will be fulfilling and successful. The vision of the Three of Wands seen in the moon, show us the potential future that lies ahead, where all the ingredients needed for a promising start to a new venture are in place.

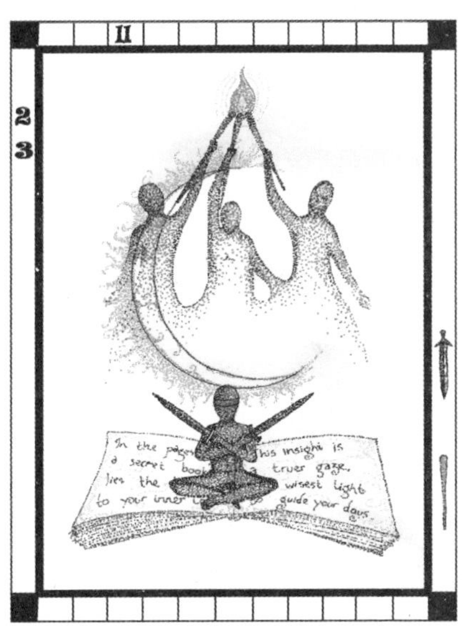

The High Priestess is designed to combine particularly well with the Magician, as she is his female counterpart.

III-The Empress

In most traditional decks, The Empress is represented as a throned female figure, surrounded by the fruits of nature and seemingly bursting forth with life. More often than not, she is pregnant, her ripening belly reflecting the fertility of the natural world around her. Other traditional symbols include a crown of stars, an orb, a field of wheat, and the planetary symbol for Venus.

In order to find the simplest way to depict this card, I did not have to look far to see the essential meaning I needed to convey. All of the above symbols pointed to essentially the same thing—Mother Nature. As the Major Arcana are intended to be the landscapes on which the Minor Arcana play out their lives, this was one of the cards that lent itself to the idea perfectly and naturally, without any strain of conceptualization on my part. The rolling hills, blue sky, and blossoming flowers sum up in the simplest way the gentle, giving, and eternally enduring nature of the Empress. She is the archetypal Mother, the great Goddess who loves and gives unconditionally to her children. The Empress is the womb from which we are born, the breast that gives forth our milk, and the green and fertile land that supports our every step.

Divinatory Meaning

Individually within a reading, the Empress suggests the unconditional and nurturing love of a mother. This may be the querent, a figure in their life, or a general atmosphere about their life. Of all the cards, she is most likely to speak of fertility and potential childbirth. More abstractly, there is a protective and stable landscape here, in which new ideas can develop and grow. The Empress encourages us to be patient with our creativity. If we give a new enterprise time, attention and care, it may grow into a beautiful baby.

However, it is important to remember the darker side of motherhood. If you should find this card reversed, it may indicate the smothering and irrational energy of the overbearing or over anxious mother. Unfortunately, it can also indicate problems in pregnancy or childbirth.

In combination with other cards, the Empress brings a feminine and receptive quality. The Empress may slow down the events of a reading, encouraging us to be patient and to let things develop naturally. She brings fertility to partnerships, families and new ventures, and a caring soul for those in need.

Here is an example of a three-card combination featuring the Empress:

Here we see the Empress as a backdrop for the Two of Wands and the King of Cups. The Wands card shows a passionate debate and the need to choose between two directions. Perhaps it is the start of a new business partnership, or the querent is in two minds himself over which path is best. The King of Cups seems to loom gently over the fiery wands, and indicates clearly which side he favors. He is a mature figure of great emotional depth and wisdom, and it would be prudent to follow his guidance! Along with the gentle yet powerful energy of the Empress in the reading, it is clear that a patient and caring response is needed. The Empress here shows us that there does not need to be haste in the decision making process, but to take time to find the true insight of the King of Cups, and follow your inner wisdom.

The Empress is the female counterpart to the Emperor, the next card in the sequence of the Major Arcana, and so they are designed to compliment each other perfectly.

IV-The Emperor

Whilst the Empress stands for the world of nature and the nurturing instincts of a mother, the Emperor stands for the man-made world and the discipline of a father. A city sky-line seems far removed from the traditional image of the throned Emperor, scepter and orb in hand, wearing his fiery red robe and armor, but as a symbol, it communicates much the same idea. It seemed logical to juxtapose the gentle landscape of the Empress with a constructed and imposing cityscape for her counterpart. The city is a place of rules, order, ambition and structure—all areas ruled by the Emperor. Within that order lies a very different kind of beauty, but who isn't awed by the sight of an illuminated city at night?

With the Emperor there is a sense of directed creative energy, which is focused under one leader. Unlike the natural process of the Empress, this is the sort of creation that works to plans, diagrams, and deadlines, with the increased pressure and sense of urgency that this implies, but with impressive re-sults. In this sense, the Emperor could be seen as the architect of his own being.

The Emperor offers stability based on structure, and will treat fairly those who abide by his rules and authority. As a leader, he rules with wisdom and charisma, in total control of everything that surrounds him. The skyscrapers, with their an-gular and dominating presence express the masculinity of the energy of this card, providing a complement and contrast to the feminine, undulating hills of the Empress. The Emperor, like a city, can promise great things, but also like a city, can be harsh and cruel. Some people thrive in an environment of control and stability, particularly if they are the one in control, whilst others find it stifling. Likewise initial reactions to the Emperor within a reading tend to vary from individual to individual.

Divinatory Meaning

When the Emperor appears in a reading he brings the power of leadership and control. If he represents the querent, it is time for them to take charge of their life and be the one giving the orders for once! Provided he is upright, he exudes the qualities of a benevolent leader or caring father, bringing life into order with a firm but fair hand. He speaks of direct action with no time for introspection or intuition. The Emperor advises us to be confident, active, and bold in our decisions and lifestyle.

If he is reversed, then we are presented with the dark side of the city. Think about the boss that everyone hates but is too scared to argue with, and you have a classic case of Emperor reversed. It is important in this case to look at your own life and ask if it is you who have become the tyrant, and think about ways to change this pattern. When power is hoarded or clung to, it can become very unhealthy indeed, for all concerned.

The Emperor could also appear in a reading to represent a figure of influence in the querent's life, perhaps a father or other authority figure, or else the environment that the querent finds him or herself in. Again, if he appears upright he can be a rock of stability, but reversed there is likely to be trouble. The Emperor in his purest form is power, and misplaced power can be the cause of great suffering. As an example you can look at any country that has lived in the shadow of a tyrannical dictator.

Within a combination, the Emperor brings a quality of order and control, encouraging us to tackle any problems head on and not to put up with any rubbish! His energy, provided it is positively aspected, will give the power needed to overcome most obstacles. Negatively aspected, he will most likely be the source of any problems himself.

Here is an example of a three-card combination featuring the Emperor:

At the bottom of the image we see the deject-ed figure of the Five of Cups, with the seemingly pinned down Eight of Swords towering over the Emperor's city. Initial im-pressions seem to speak of an emotional personality that feels trapped by a disciplined environment. This almost seems liter-ally to be someone who has tried to make it in the city and has failed. But if we look deeper into this image, there is a more positive side. There has

been an immediate problem, shown by the two fallen cups, and it is that problem that is keeping the querent trapped in a feeling of loss and solitude. But behind the sitting figure are three more upright cups, holding the promise of brighter things in the future. The swords surrounding the standing figure are problems conjured by the mind, which she will be able to fight through when she realizes that the power of the Emperor is at her disposal. So after a time of struggle and despondency, if the querent can find their inner Emperor and take control for themselves, the problems can eventually be conquered.

As her male counterpart, the Emperor is designed to combine perfectly with the Empress.

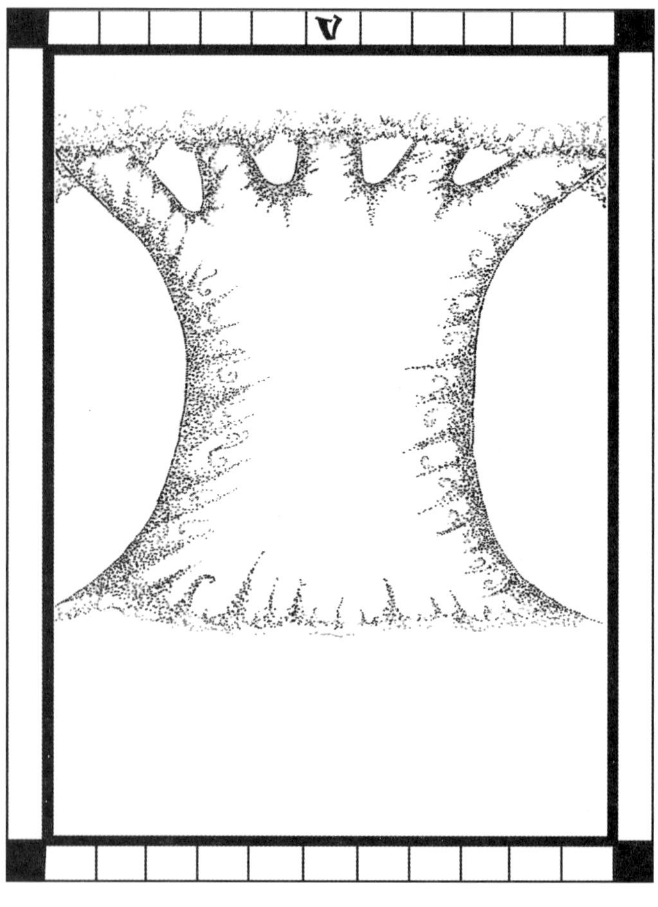

V-The Hierophant

This image of an ancient oak, with its roots reaching deep into the earth and strong branches raised to the heavens may again seem greatly removed from the traditional Tarot imagery, but the symbolic message that it communicates is much the same. Those who are familiar with other Tarot decks will be used to the image of an imposing papal figure preaching to two highly attentive acolytes. It is obvious from his appearance that he is concerned with ancient traditions and laws, and passing them down to his loyal and conscientious students.

Often though, to those uncomfortable with established or conventional religions, the priestly appearance of this card can evoke a negative reaction, making it difficult to see his positive aspects. Where the High Priestess encourages us to turn inward in the search for the spiritual, the Hierophant's purpose is to bring the spiritual down to earth. He is a wise and patient teacher, though he may seem stuck in his ways, because of his earthy nature. The simplified symbol of the oak tree is immediately reminiscent of an earth-based spirituality, its delving roots reflecting the fixed yet growing nature of tradition, its great branches signifying a connection to the higher realms of spirit. The foliage of the great tree represents the knowledge to be shared, as well as a place to shelter from the ravages of the world.

Imagine in the many centuries of an oak's life, all the many events it has witnessed, and how we could benefit from that knowledge. The wisdom of the tree, the teacher of wisdom that comes from the very earth herself, is ours to share if we can learn to listen and attend like the acolytes of the Hierophant.

Divinatory Meaning

The Hierophant often stands for a teacher or advisor when he appears in a reading. If he appears to represent the querent, then it may be that it is time for them to take on the mantle of the teacher for themselves, their knowledge having reached the level where they are ready to share it with others. In this case, he not only speaks of being part of a great tradition, but also reminds us to keep our feet well and truly on the ground! Although, because of his fixed nature, the Hierophant can appear stubborn, even 'stuffy', (he stands for the zodiac sign of Taurus), he is always trustworthy and has ancient wisdom to share with those who have the patience to listen.

In his worst aspect, the Hierophant has lost the ability to translate the wisdom to his students and becomes almost a dictator of the law. If this refers to the querent, it could be time to look at old habits and bossy tendencies and try to loosen up a little. If the Hierophant reversed is a person in the querent's life, beware of false gurus and poor, unworthy teachers. It may mean a time to break free from tradition and move into a new mode of living and belief.

Here is an example of a three-card combination featuring the Hierophant:

The Hierophant clearly dominates this image, with the dazed figure of the Seven of Cups to one side and the guardian-like Nine of Wands poised protectively in front. Perhaps there is a temptation to stray from traditional values, shown in the many cups presented to the less stable figure. Dazzled by the seemingly more glamorous options, he could be easily led from his true path. The Nine of Wands however, seems more aware of the illusory nature of these choices, and is firmly planted in a defensive stance before the great tree of the Hierophant. This combination seems to be advising the querent that although new choices may seem appealing, there is great value to be found in the old and familiar. Be open to new learning, but not overwhelmed by it, and be ready to stand by what you truly believe. The oak tree can support you when you need shelter, and stabilize you when you feel unbalanced, just as true wisdom and faith can. The time may come when you are called to similarly defend your beliefs in return, not through aggression, but by confidence and assurance in where your truth lies. Within this it is important to realize that your truth is not necessarily the same as the truth of others, and do not fall prey to the more stubborn side of the Hierophant. This is sometimes a thin line to tread.

The Hierophant combines particularly well with the High Priestess and the Hermit, the other spiritual teachers of the deck. Together they may teach us to listen not only with our ears to the great teachers, but with our heart and soul.

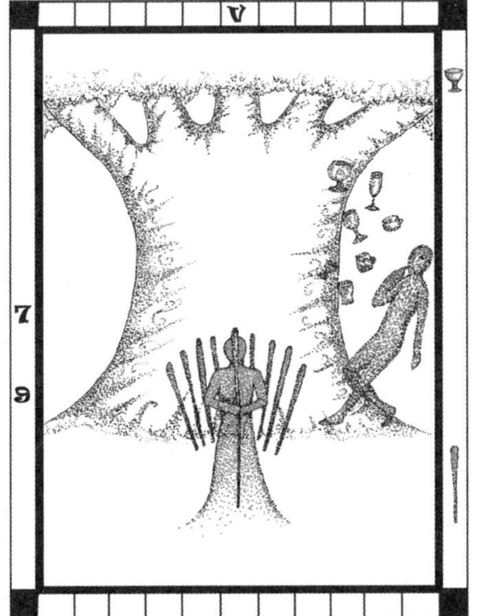

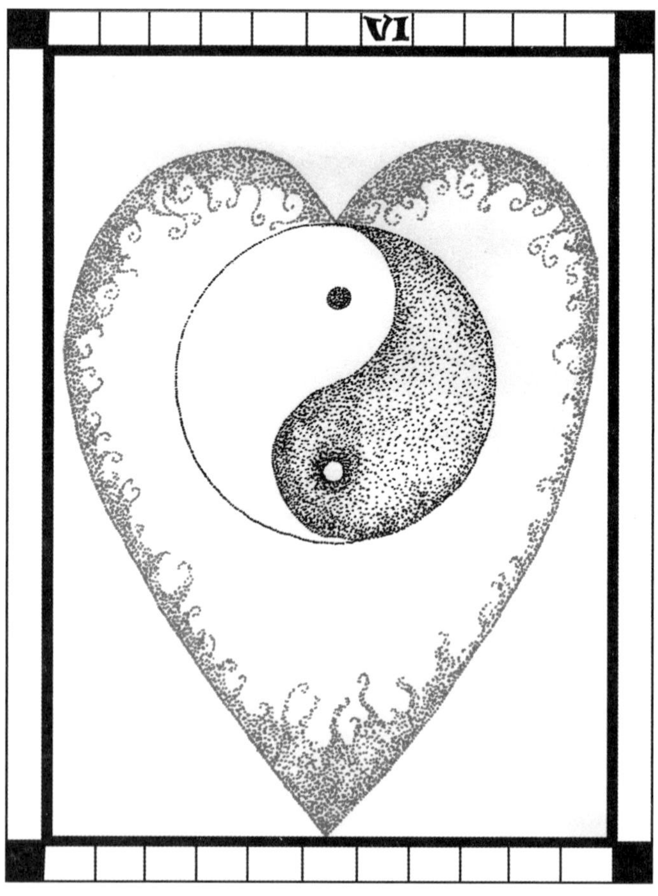

VI-The Lovers

This card encapsulates the ideal partnership, where two halves find each other and join in perfect balance. Conventionally, this card shows a marriage arranged by heavenly forces, with a male and female figure, (or sometimes a male and two females), Cupid aiming his bow, and sometimes a priest. It is an image that instantly conveys the message of love and commitment, and that spiritual forces are at work in their union. It was not difficult to distill this idea down into one striking symbol—the ancient Chinese Yin-Yang surrounded by a red heart.

Most of us are familiar with the joined symbol of Yin and Yang. Although it generally represents the greater universal pattern of opposite and complementary forces coming together in balance, it is also a very apt symbol for a relationship between soul mates. The dark, receptive, intuitive, and feminine Yin joins with the solar, active, rational, and masculine Yang to form the perfect circle, each containing a small element of the other. Here the symbol is surrounded by the instantly-recognizable red heart, showing that this perfection is brought about through love and for love's purpose.

Divinatory Meaning

The most obvious meaning when the Lovers appears in a reading is that of a new relationship or love interest, or a new commitment within an existing relationship. There are, however, many other possibilities. Instead of a partner, this card may speak about finding this perfect balance of forces within yourself, and hence a renewed love of life. It may also speak about finding the perfect business partner with which to pursue a career that you truly love, or indeed, the perfect career itself. It can also speak of the need to make a commitment, as in a marriage or other contract. It often speaks of the need to make a choice, and commit to that choice, or can simply remind us that we have free will to choose as we please. As with any card, the meaning will become most clear through the use of your intuition, and through the combinations with other cards. For instance, if combined with the Four of Wands, it almost definitely speaks of a marriage and setting up a new home with a great love. If the Ace of Pentacles were to appear, it would most likely mean a wonderful new career, and so on. The key meaning is that of two elements coming together as one and becoming greater than the sum of their parts.

If the Lovers appears reversed in a reading, then harmony has been lost, or a commitment is faltering. This may signify disloyalty, an affair or other betrayal, or it may mean simply a loss of balance within the self. The Lovers reversed can be a spiteful force of retaliation, with sweeter memories tainted by thoughts of vengeance. Again, it is crucial to listen to your inner voice, and look to other cards in the combination for clarification.

Here is an example of a three-card combination featuring the Lovers:

Rarely could a combination sing 'soul mate' as much as this! Here the Two of Cups meet together in the centre of the Yin-Yang symbol, their cups joined in mutual recognition as a toast to their new love. Everything in this image is aligned and in balance as the light of illumination shines from the Hermit's mountain top. They seem literally to be floating on cloud nine and are surrounded by the great red heart of the Lovers card. The Hermit's energy combined with the Lovers and the Two of Cups means this is very much a spiritual match with a good chance of lasting through any trials that lie ahead. Their meeting is a step forward on their mutual spiritual path, and they will be able to grow together as one united. Together they will make discoveries and uncover talents that would have lain dormant as individuals, and become a shining example to others in every aspect of their life together. A joyous combination indeed!

The Lovers is designed to fit particularly well with the Two of Cups, but also with the World, the Moon, the Sun, and the Star—all the cosmic forces. You will also notice how well it fits with the Devil card—a warning of how we can become entrapped by desire of the physical aspect of love.

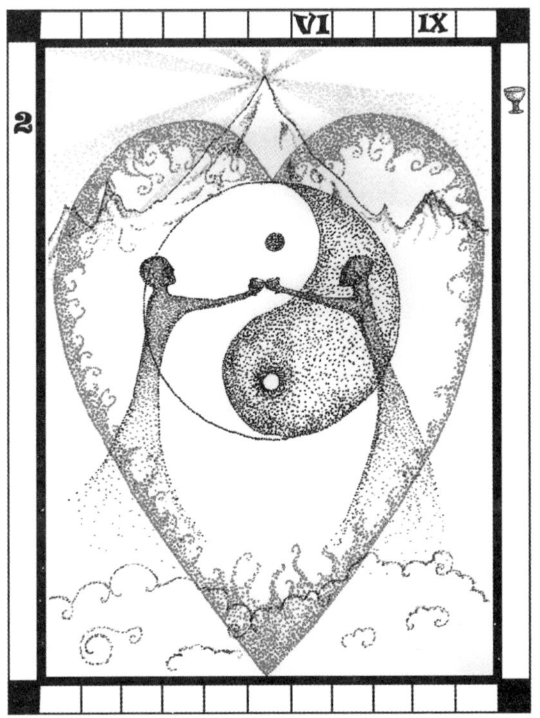

VII-The Chariot

The Chariot can appear to be quite a puzzling card, for although one of the things it signifies is motion, most traditional decks show the Chariot sitting perfectly still! This is a card of opposites, contradictions, conflicts and their integration; hence the black and white horses of this card. These horses, or sometimes a pair of sphinxes or other beasts, also appear on most conventional renderings of this card, in addition to an armored figure, the chariot itself, and a starry canopy. Each of these symbols has a good deal of significance, so it was important to get to the heart of the card to find a single symbol to evoke its meaning. The two horses are trying to head in opposite directions, but are shown to come from the same source. They symbolize the various elements within our lives that must be tamed and brought into alignment before real progress can be made. The horse is a powerful animal, and can be difficult to control, particularly as it has a mind of its own. However, once harnessed, that power, (in this case of *two* horses), can bring great momentum and victory.

All of us at some point in our lives have experienced a feeling of being overwhelmed by the many seemingly conflicting demands on our time, as though we are spinning plates, or juggling many tasks at once. The Chariot not only represents the ability to balance these elements, but also to harness their momentum and use that power to succeed in life. A necessary part of that success is the development of a confident persona with which to face society, and it is through the inherent struggle to achieve cohesion between all the conflicting elements without and within that bring that confidence to the fore.

Divinatory Meaning

If it was necessary to sum up the meaning of this card in one word, it would be 'victory'. However, this is not the easily won or gifted type of victory, but rather one that comes as a great reward after a lengthy period of struggle. The Chariot's appearance in a reading signifies a new mastery over parts of life that may have previously been in conflict. This card is a sign that the querent has made a conscious decision not to be a victim of circumstance, and has not only turned things around for the better, but has made the difficulties actually work to his or her advantage. The chaotic elements of life, like wild horses, have been tamed, becoming the very thing that brings momentum and positive change into the querent's life. In many ways, this card can be a complex element in a reading, because it not only speaks of a chain of events rather than a single event or energy, but also the results of those events. Once we realize we can take the reins of life into our own hands, there is a self-assurance and confidence that is rooted not in arrogance, but in true knowledge of our inner strength and abilities.

When the Chariot is negatively aspected, however, there may be a tendency to dominate or even bully others into agreement. Instead of well-earned victory, it becomes the unbalanced campaign of the tyrant. Another possible interpretation of this card's reversed meaning is a loss of control and confidence which was previously in place. As always it depends on the placement in the reading and the other cards in the combination.

Here is an example of a three-card combination featuring the Chariot:

Here the power of the Chariot supports the figure of the Two of Pentacles as he juggles his many responsibilities, and the Eight of Wands as he races forwards to face the future. Within this combination we can see clearly the daily struggle of balancing the many factors of daily life and the need to take control in order to move forward. The two pentacles balanced in the figure's hands are echoed in the two

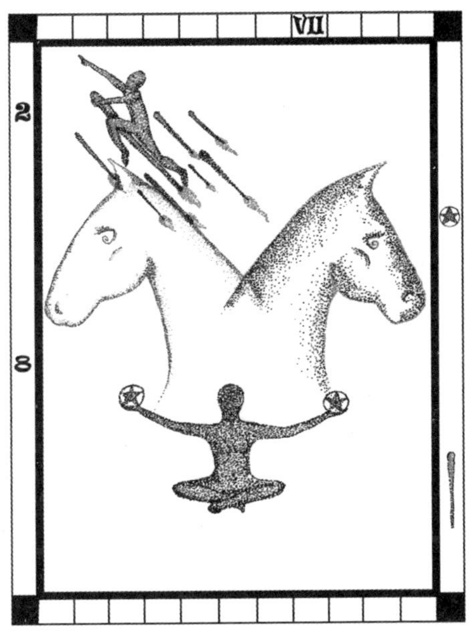

horses of the Chariot, which would imply that the integration of these seemingly opposing forces will be successful. In the Eight of Wands, with the figure riding the energy almost like a witch's broomstick, we can see the result of this victorious endeavor and further confirmation that rapid and confident progress will be made due to the harnessing of this power.

The Chariot and the Six of Wands are designed to work particularly well together as they both signify victory.

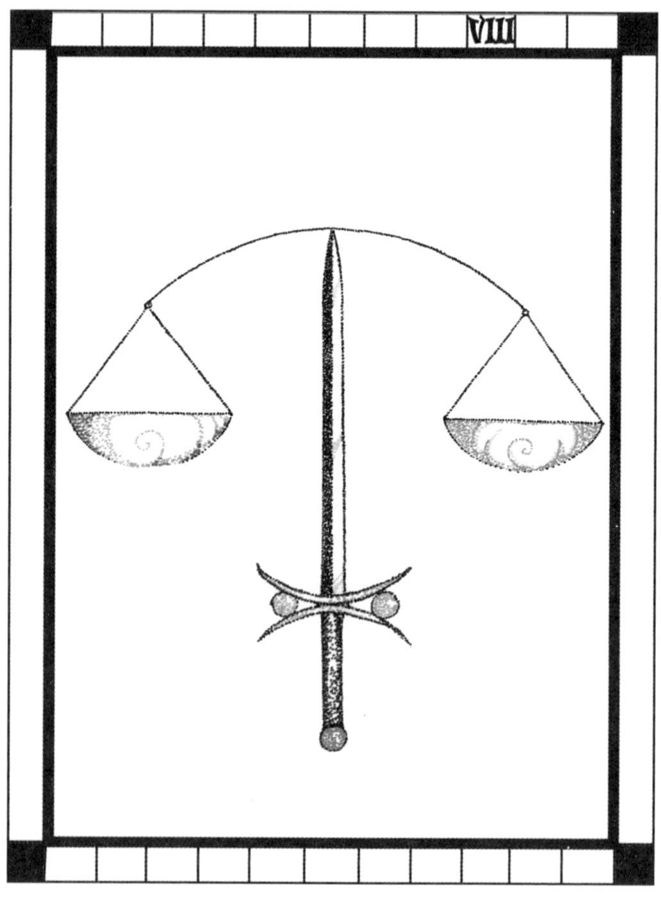

VIII-Justice

Justice as she appears in most traditional Tarot decks is a familiar figure in many cultures. She is almost always seen as a dignified woman with a regal bearing, holding a sword in one hand, and scales in the other. Quite often, the figure of Justice wears a blindfold to symbolize her emotional detachment and objectivity, and the need to look within to find the truth. In this rendering of the card, the familiar symbols of the sword and scales have been combined into one, the scales balancing precariously on the sharp tip of the blade. These two symbols have been intimately associated with the concept of justice for many centuries, probably since the objects themselves came into being.

The scales have been used to symbolize justice as far back as Ancient Egypt, when it was believed that our souls were weighed against the weight of a feather after death, with unattoned sins causing the scales to tip. It is an appropriate symbol indeed for the workings of justice, as the tiniest event or piece of information can be key in seeing justice, or indeed *in*justice done. On a more universal level, the scales represent the need for balance within ourselves, between the many conflicting aspects of personality that we start to discover as we mature, and the increasing demands on our time and energies. The scales on this card consist of a silver bowl on one side, representing the lunar, or internal self, and a golden bowl, signifying the solar, or external self. If we exist in balance, we are capable of dealing with the tasks laid before us. When we live in imbalance, even the smallest segment of daily life can become a strain.

The sword, like the scales, is also two sided and in balance—or rather, it is double-edged. It is the sword of Justice that displays her authority, and dispenses the appropriate punishment. Like the sword, any punishment will always be double-edged, for what seems Justice to one, may be judged unfair suffering by another.

Divinatory Meaning

When Justice appears in a reading, the truth will out! Her sword pierces the veil of illusion and reveals the inner workings beneath. For those with nothing to hide, Justice offers just rewards and recognition of accomplishments. On the other hand, if there are less noble deeds that have been buried, Justice will see that due punishment is received. Like the universal workings of Karma that she represents, Justice acts impersonally and wisely.

She can, for obvious reasons, often represent a court case or other dealings with the legal system. Again, it not only depends on the situation of the querent, but on the orientation of the card as to the outcome of such dealings. Generally, if she is upright, then the result will favor whichever party is in the right.

She may also appear in a reading in a more spiritual capacity, urging us to seek the balance within. Her sword can aid us in slaying many old demons as we bring light to our shadow selves and acknowledge the shadow cast by the light. She reminds us to be aware of the workings of Karma within our lives, and that we receive that which we give out, whether it be good or bad.

On those occasions when justice may appear reversed, the interpretation may be literally '*in*justice'. Unfair events may plague the querent, or perhaps they themselves are getting away with something that they should be facing in the open. Spiritually, when Justice is reversed, the inner and outer realms are out of balance. This must be addressed, as imbalance can often lead to illness, both mental and/or physical.

Here is an example of a three-card combination featuring Justice:

Here the scales of Justice support the luxurious figure of the Nine of Pentacles, and seem to loom over the reticent Four of Cups. The solar side of the scales seems satisfied, with the Nine of Pentacles draped comfortably within the bowl, admiring her belongings and material accomplishments. However, below the surface, the Four of Cups looks unhappy with her lot, seeking more in life, as the

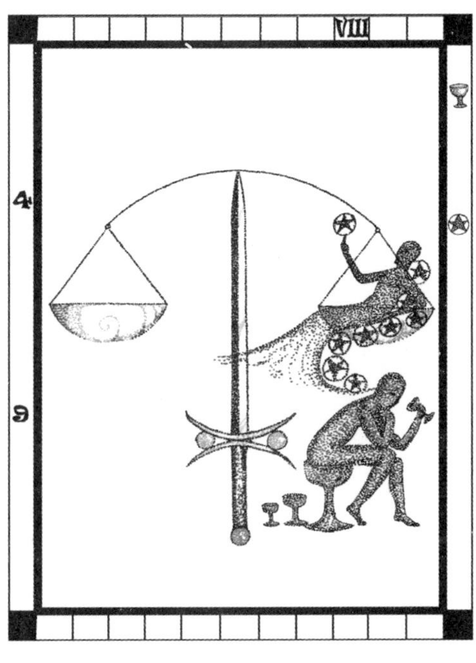

lunar side of the scales remains empty. In order to address this seeming imbalance of life, the querent may benefit from time spent exploring the inner realms, and finding deeper meaning behind the workings of life. Without that, even the fullest cup can still seem empty.

Justice is designed to combine particularly well with The Chariot, and Temperance as they are all images that speak of inner balance, but she also combines well with all the other cards, as she is a force that is constantly at work in our lives.

IX- The Hermit

The Hermit is portrayed in most decks as a solitary, robed figure, carrying a staff and lantern. As he strides forward into the night, his lantern illuminates the path and dispels any lurking shadows. In many ways, the Hermit is closely related to the Fool, as both are spiritual seekers, but as the Fool sees with the eyes of a child, the Hermit is the ancient wise man who walks steadily and sees all. Where the Fool finds wisdom through his blind leap of faith, the Hermit shines his light clearly and supports each step with his sturdy staff, wrought of experience.

The Hermit calls for a time of solitude and introspection, and it is this primary meaning which inspired the symbolism of this card. An ancient mountain towers high above the clouds, a mysterious yet penetrating light radiating from its peak. Beneath the cloud may be found more mundane matters, and the everyday world, but the great mountain stands apart from that world, quite literally absorbed in higher matters. Although the mountain itself appears quite still, it inspires many to climb its slopes to learn the great lessons that are found not only in the destination, but most importantly in the journey itself. There are many paths up the mountain, just as there are many paths to spiritual enlightenment, and the Hermit encourages us to find our own. In ancient tales from many spiritual traditions, the great teacher may be found at the highest point of the mountain, with valuable insights and answers to the seeker's questions. As in Buddhist teachings, any of us are capable of achieving this enlightenment, our wisdom shining from the mountain peak like a great beacon, illuminating the path for all.

Divinatory meaning

When the Hermit represents the querent in a reading, it is time to look within for answers, retreating for a while from the outside world and all its distractions. It is through this isolation and reflection that great insights may come, and spiritual revelations. The Hermit displays not a 'love and light' sort of spirituality, but a willingness to explore the shadows, and bring hidden gems of wisdom into the light of day. His need for solitude may sometimes seem strange to others, and can also manifest as a lack of patience with any who interrupt his peace. If the querent is an artist or writer, the Hermit represents exactly the sort of state they must be in to receive their essential inspiration.

In questions of relationships, there is a sense of loneliness inherent in this card. Perhaps someone feels isolated within the relationship, or they wish to break out on their own for a while. The Hermit can often indicate the desire for one's own space and time alone.

Of course, the Hermit may also represent an important person in the life of the querent, such as a spiritual teacher or inspirational figure. Because they stand apart from normal society, this sort of person can seem eccentric and does not socialize well, but they have many insights to share with those who will listen.

The Hermit may also appear in a reading when you are pursuing a course of study that takes you deeper into your hidden self and furthers you along your path in a challenging and fulfilling way.

In a combined image, the Hermit brings a sense of peace and spirituality. However, if he should appear reversed, then solitude is difficult to find and signals from spirit may be blocked. The mundane world has taken over and spiritual learning has taken a back seat. The Hermit reversed is also a likely card to appear when dealing with a false guru who is interested only in monetary gain and the exploitation of the needs of others.

Here is an example of a three-card combination featuring The Hermit:

Here the Hermit is providing the backdrop for the creative Page of Pentacles and the sneaky Seven of Swords. The Page is running across the surface of the clouds, pleased with the pentacle she carries, which may be either a new creation or payment for a job well done. However, above her head the thief-like figure of the Seven of Swords seems to be making off in a hurry with that which has not been so rightfully earned. As the Hermit shines his all pervading light on this situation, it must be an opportunity for spiritual learning. The young and eager Page of Pentacles may be well advised to keep her new treasure to herself, lest someone attempts to take credit for her work. The Seven of Swords often indicates events behind the scenes that although they affect the querent, are not yet apparent to her. Once the Page's creative ideas are fully formed and mature, then she will become the wise Hermit herself and may be able to teach the opportunistic thief the errors of his ways.

The Hermit Combines particularly well with the High Priestess and the Fool, as well as being a wonderful comple-ment to most other cards in the deck.

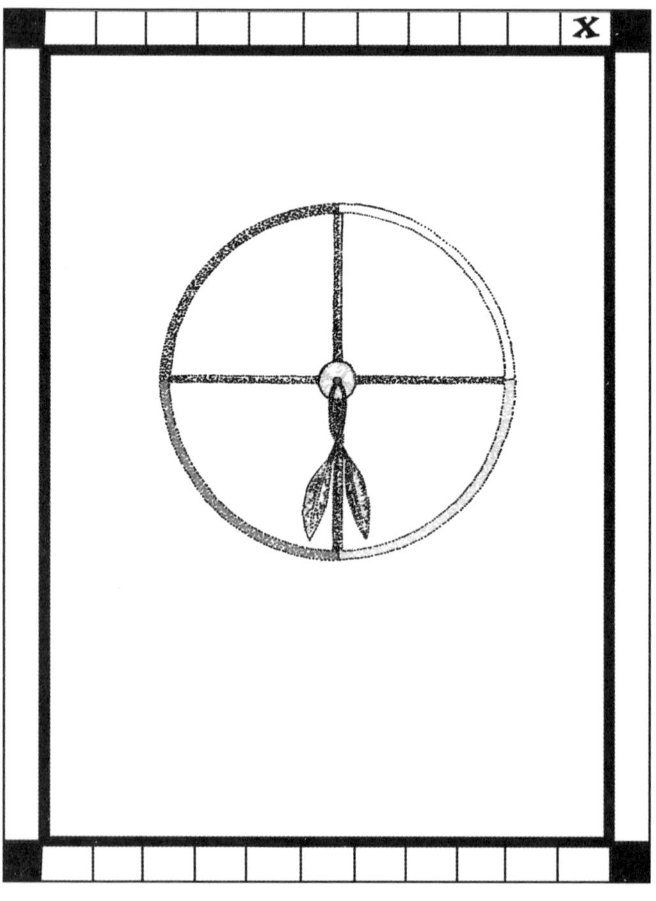

X-The Wheel

Unlike most traditional decks, there is no complex array of mythical beasts on show in this card. Instead, the forces of fate and chance are here represented by a Native American medicine wheel, a symbol of harmony and the cycles of nature. The four directions indicated by the segments of the circle not only represent the four elements of earth, air, fire and water, but also the seasons and forces through which we and the world travel. Within these four directions are also contained all creatures, plants, and races of the planet, according to the season and element that they are aligned with. In short, it is a simplified version of the web of life itself. As we move through the seasons and elemental forces ebb and flow within us, so there are times when we seem gifted by these forces with good fortune. It is these times of which this card speaks.

The Wheel represents that force which on the simplest level we think of as 'luck'. The forces of fate can appear inexplicable and random, sometimes leaving us changed forever. A stroke of luck can seem like a completely random bolt from the blue, whereas there may in fact be many undetected ripples leading up to the event. On a deeper level, we can see this as the workings of the web of life, and though it may seem mystifying to us as our view is limited to our own existence, as part of the bigger picture, it has a harmonious place.

The Wheel rules over all such events that seem engineered by fate or mysterious forces, and though it normally brings good fortune, the same forces can also bring what seems to be misfortune. In this case we must remember that there is growth and learning to be found in all situations, and that if it is the weaving of the web that has brought such happenings, there must be a higher purpose.

Divinatory Meaning

When the Wheel appears in a reading, then it usually means that higher forces are at work in the life of the querent. It can represent something as simple and mundane as finding or winning a much-needed sum of money, or something as life changing as getting a great new job or meeting a person who will become a key influence. It almost goes without saying that when we are open to the idea of positive events occurring in our lives and look out for potential opportunities, then they are more likely to occur. If the Wheel has made its presence known to you, then it is a good time to ask the universe for what you need, for someone is sure to be listening.

As a part of a combination, the Wheel brings an optimistic edge to any events, showing that fate is at work, even though it may seem to be in mysterious ways.

If the Wheel should appear to be reversed or negatively aspected, it would be prudent to brace yourself for a run of bad luck. Remember though, that like any rough winter, misfortune will pass and spring will come again.

Here is an example of a three-card combination featuring The Wheel:

Here the Ace of Swords seems to penetrate the Wheel as, in one quarter of its circle, the Six of Cups sweetly reminisces. Overall, this appears to be a very balanced and positive combination. The Ace emerging from the bottom right speaks of mental clarity, new communications and a fresh start. As the Wheel is the major influence here, then it seems likely that this breath of fresh air is a fated event or meeting. As the Six of Cups is associated with fond memories and happy childhood, perhaps this may be a new contact with an old friend or relative who was thought lost? As the sword points clearly at the more adult of the two figures, it seems likely that a person whom the querent looked up to and trusted in the past will suddenly make a new and welcome appearance in their life. It could also mean that new knowledge about events from the past will come to light that will bring great happiness and a new perspective to the querent.

The Wheel is designed to combine well with the World, as they have many traits in common, and also mixes well with the Sun, the Moon, the Devil, and the Star.

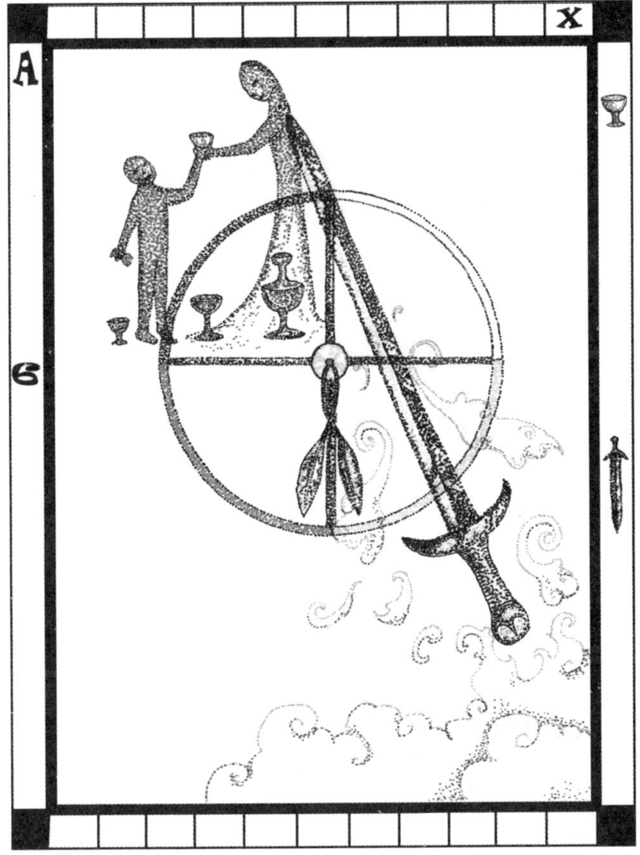

XI-Strength

It has been remarked that this card has many similarities in meaning to the Chariot, as both cards deal with the subject of mastery of self, confidence, and exertion of willpower. However, the feel of this card, which follows closely the traditional symbolism of the maiden who has tamed the wild beast, (normally a lion), seems far more gentle and spiritual compared to the dynamic nature of the Chariot. Although you cannot see the maiden's eyes in this card, you can sense the intimate contact between her soul and the panther's spirit.

Whereas the Chariot tends to signify control and victory over conflicting *external* elements, this far more feminine card is more likely to speak of the spiritual victory over conflicting elements and feelings *within* the self. Strength signifies one of the most important lessons on any spiritual path, and that is to 'know thyself'.

Through self-knowledge we are able to identify and integrate our inner beast or shadow self and manifest it constructively in our lives, rather than seeing it as something to be feared and buried. This also builds a strong connection between this card and the Magician, as 'Know Thyself' is one of the prime tenets of ritual magick.

Learning how to tame our inner demons rather than constantly battle them can be the challenge of a lifetime, but the benefits can be seen clearly in this card. Rather than wasting energy and giving away power with our internal struggles, we can bring ourselves into alignment under one unifying force—the will. Once we truly know our inner beast and have gained its trust and companionship, we have not only renewed confidence, but are no longer exhausting ourselves by suppressing a source of power. Rather we can call on it when needed, and then, under the leadership of our willpower, we can be strong indeed.

Divinatory Meaning

The Strength card brings a wonderful feeling of calm self-assurance to any reading. The incredible look of unbreakable trust in the big cat's eyes is reflected in our own feelings when we see this card. It seems to tell us that whatever may be transpiring in life, not to worry, for we have the strength to see it through with dignity and compassion. Strength shows the ability to remain calm in any situation and turn it to our advantage. It does not tend to represent physical strength, but rather the inner strength of the spiritual warrior. As the maiden's inner strength and conviction can gain the trust and allegiance of the wild beast, so we can face all the challenges life can throw at us and use them to make us stronger still.

If the Strength card should appear reversed or negatively aspected in a reading, great care must be taken not to allow yourself to be ruled by the inner beast. Primal impulses may seem overpowering, threatening to defeat the higher self and de-throne willpower. Strength reversed indicates a time of chaotic loss of control and an almost schizophrenic fragmentation of personality. A great force of will and much spiritual work must be undertaken to bring the personality back into balance and regain control of all aspects of the self.

Here is an example of a three-card combination featuring Strength:

In this combination, Strength gently dominates the centre of the image, whilst the Knight of Wands kneels poised in the foreground, and the Ten of Swords seems a background memory. Certainly the Ten shows that the querent has endured difficult times, and may well feel mentally and emotionally exhausted at the end of these trials. However, the hard times have now finally come to an end, and through the pain and loss, great spiritual lessons have been learnt. It seems the realization that it is futile to battle with the self has been made, and it is time for a new approach. The presence of the Strength card here shows us that when we feel we have nothing left, we still have the spark of our soul. That spark of spirit may be kindled through increased self-awareness and manifest in the boundless energy of the Knight of Wands. Although this particular court card can sometimes have a reckless and unpredictable nature, the influence of Strength will assure that his energy is properly channeled and controlled by the supreme power of the will.

Strength combines particularly well with the Hermit, the High Priestess, and the Magician, as they all deal with different aspects of spiritual self-mastery.

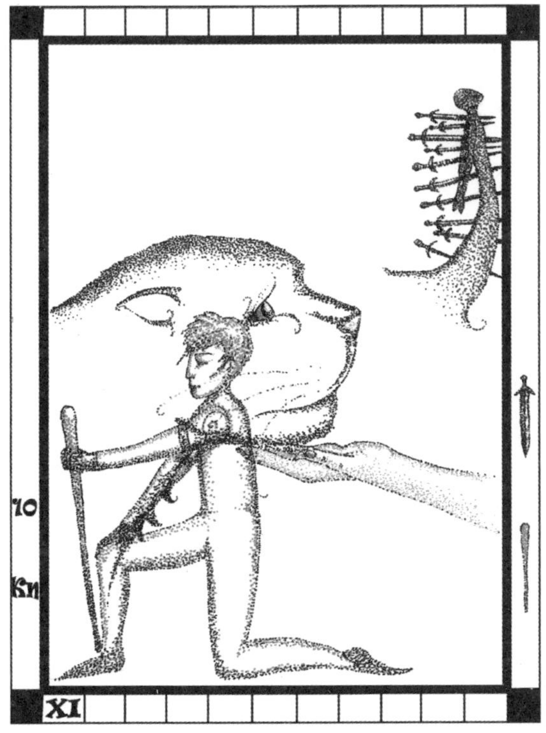

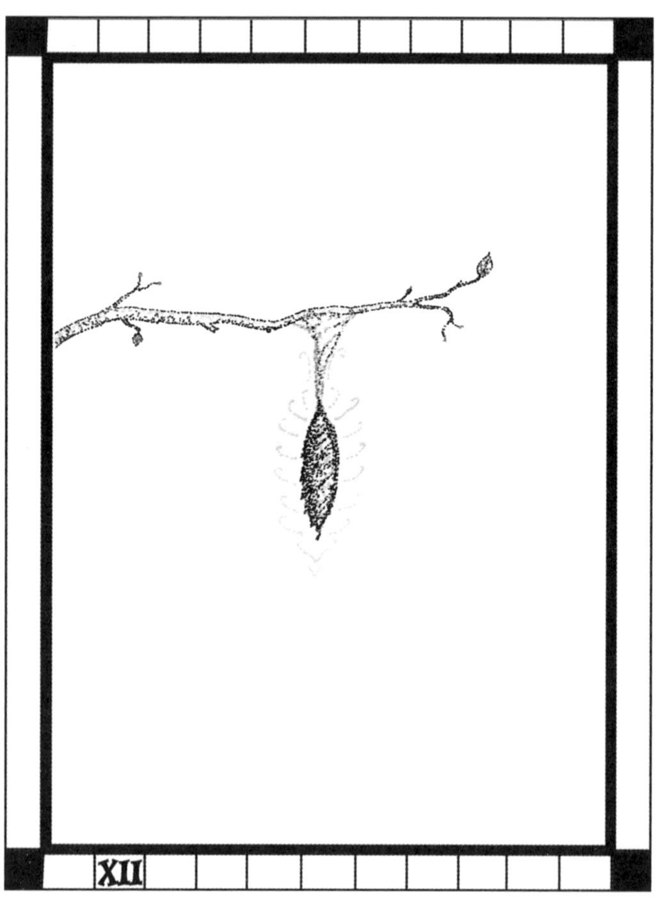
XII

XII-The Hanged One

This card is more traditionally known as 'The Hanged Man', as it normally depicts a man suspended from a branch by his ankle, his head surrounded by a halo of inspiration. To those well versed in mythology, this image instantly brings to mind the tale of the Norse god Odin, and the means by which he gained the sacred runes. Legend tells us that he hung from the great tree of life, Yggdrasil, for nine days and nights, his side pierced by his own spear, until the runes appeared beneath him and he was able to gather their power and share their wisdom with the world. Within this tale and imagery can be found many clues as to the depth of meaning of this card.

'The Hanged Man', or in this case 'The Hanged One', teaches us not only the power of self-sacrifice, but also the wisdom that can be gained through a change of perspective and a temporary removal of everyday distractions. Those who seek true wisdom know that there must often be a sacrifice made, but that the wisdom gained will always be fair payment. Within native shamanic practices across the globe, there are many examples of people pushing themselves physically to the limits in order to transcend the physical altogether and enter an altered state. Through this sacrifice, like Odin, they can gain new wisdom and teachings to benefit not just the individual, but all who are willing and able to learn. Like the shaman, the Hanged One is suspended between two worlds and is able, through meditation and spiritual journeying, to bring knowledge from one into the other. Where the Hermit sends his light questing into the dark to dispel the shadows, the Hanged One sits in the darkness, allowing the shadows to come to him, waiting to see what will emerge.

We can only guess whether the caterpillar, as she creates her cocoon of isolation, has knowledge of the butterfly she will inevitably become, but it is a fitting symbol for the journey of inner transformation and enlightenment that this card represents. By being willing to test our endurance, deny ourselves everyday luxuries and give our spiritual selves the time and space to reflect, we can potentially uncover great gems of universal truth and emerge, like the butterfly, transformed.

Divinatory Meaning

As part of a reading, the Hanged One tells us to take a step back from unfolding events and to try to see them from a more detached perspective. It also speaks of the potential for new insights and learning, if the appropriate sacrifice is made. The gifts that are offered by the Hanged One will come to those who are patient enough to allow the butterfly its due time in the cocoon. The time to meditate and fully immerse oneself in the search for spiritual truth can be a hard thing to find in this modern world, and that is where sacrifices must be made. However, the insights gained by the Hanged One are a great gift to the world as a whole, as those of us who take the time to see the beauty around us can feel great joy at the sight of the butterfly's beautiful wings and its seemingly careless flight.

This card shows that we might feel in a state of limbo, but that important changes are happening in our inner world, while the outer world seems to be on hold. The Hanged One advises us to let events run their course, and not to try and force anything before its time. The reasons and true value of the knowledge and wisdom acquired through this process will present themselves with time.

When reversed, the Hanged One may represent impatience and an unwillingness to let events unfold naturally. It can also warn of misplaced and unnecessary sacrifice.

Here is an example of a three-card combination featuring The Hanged One:

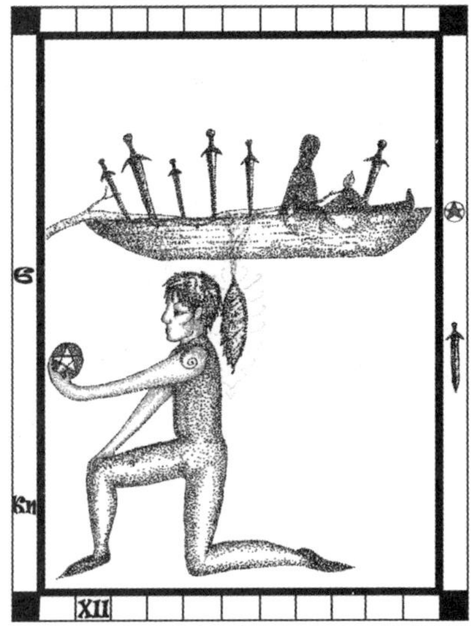

Here the branch from which the Hanged One is suspended seems almost to become the boat of the Six of Swords, and the Knight of Pentacles seems unaware of the cocoon behind his head as he kneels upon the earth. As the Six of Swords often signifies an escape from difficulties or complications, and the Knight does not seem to be able to see the answer that lies so close to him, this image suggests a soul-searching journey away from mundane distractions. This may actually be a physical journey as well as a spiritual one, through which will be gained a greater connection with, and awareness of the world. Through spending time away from the familiar and exploring new territories, new perspectives will be gained, and that which seemed faded and tired will take on new significance. It may also be that the querent will find deep connections with a new land whilst traveling, and possibly deeper understanding of a friend or partner. After all, if the Knight could but turn and face in the same direction as the boat's passenger, the lesson of the Hanged One would be staring him in the face!

The Hanged One combines well with the Hermit and Death, as it is a key stage and process between the powers represented by these two cards.

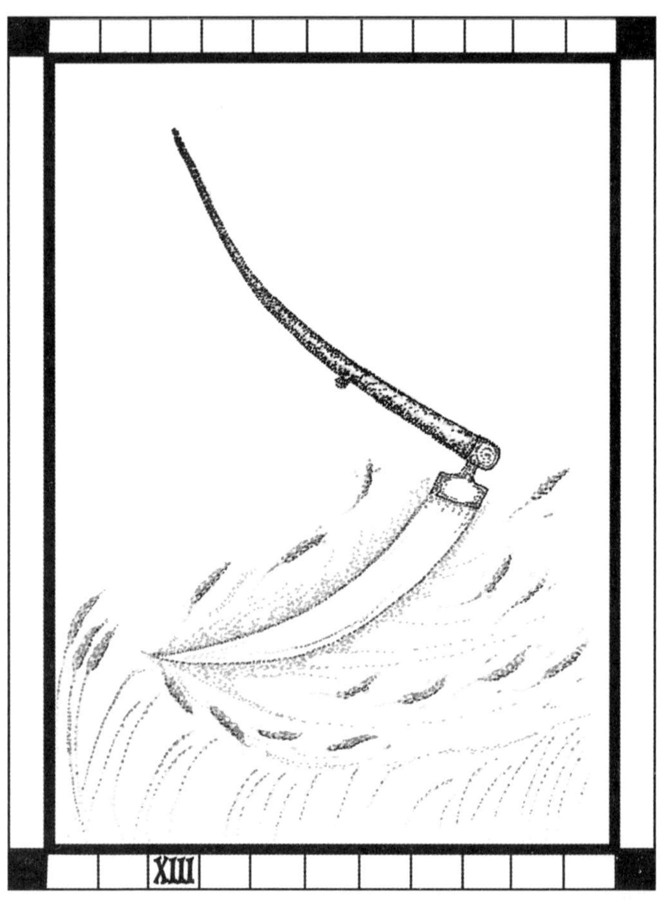
XIII

XIII-Death

Here the traditional image of the Grim Reaper cutting down victims with his scythe has been distilled down to a simpler yet derivative image of a scythe harvesting wheat. It is a less fearsome image, to be sure, and yet the meaning of the card remains unchanged. Death represents not mourning and decay, but rather an inner transformation often leading us closer to our true selves, the result of the inner spiritual work of the previous card, the Hanged One. The wheat may not be aware of the purpose for which it was planted, but it has spent much time growing to ripeness. When suddenly the harvest comes, the wheat is cut down, and may feel the loss of all that it has worked for, but the cycle must continue in order for life to flourish. Through the harvest, the wheat is used to nourish others, undergoing deep transformations into bread and other foods, fulfilling its purpose. Once it is cut down, the land is cleared again to make room for new crops in the coming year.

This is the death of which this card speaks—the loss of aspects of self or a way of life, in order to move on to another level, and new ways of being. Although this necessitates bidding farewell to fond and familiar parts of ourselves, (or in many cases not so fond), the loss is making room for new growth and life. Death leads to rebirth, and so this card speaks of the potential for an exciting new phase of life, if the old can be shed and left behind. What is buried in the ground becomes the seeds for new growth.

Divinatory Meaning

One of the most common questions about the Death card is whether it can indicate actual physical death, so it seems wise when discussing its divinatory meaning to get that question out of the way first. Yes, sometimes it can, as can several other cards in the deck. Death is an integral part of life, indeed it is the only thing we can really be certain of. If you strip away the fear however, and look at the true nature of death, particularly if you are of a spiritual nature, it is a shifting, (albeit a dramatic one), from one state into another. It is this sort of transformation that this card will represent if it appears in a reading, and it is very rare that it will be a physical death. It is wise to trust your intuition and look at the other cards in the combination to see exactly what manner of transformation it might mean, as it's likely to be different every time. For example, the Death card could appear if someone has managed to shed an old addiction or habit after many years. It could also indicate a dramatic change of career path, or graduating from school to enter adulthood. On a more spiritual level, the Death card appears when we have reached deeply into our souls and come closer to our true destiny. Often that results in great change, and is another sort of graduation! In short, to fear the Death card would be to fear change. Many people do indeed resist change in their lives, but the result can only be stagnation, for life must constantly change in order to grow.

When the Death card appears reversed in a combination, then this essential change is being resisted, with possible destructive consequences. It is far better to allow the natural progress of life than to resist its ebb and flow, otherwise what was once joyful can become bitter and stale.

Here is an example of a three-card combination featuring Death:

In this combination, the mournful Five of Cups sits amongst the wheat as the scythe of Death brings its transformative power. Behind the scythe, the Three of Cups celebrate their friendship. The Five of Cups seems a very lonely figure, absorbed in the loss of the two cups before him, which seem to have been knocked over by the scythe. These cups may well symbolize elements of the querent's life which, though missed, are better left behind. This

may be an old relationship, friendship or other emotional attachment, as cups are the rulers of emotion. However, behind the figure are three intact cups, either forgotten, or yet to be discovered. Once the wheat is cleared and the loss of the first two cups is processed, the querent will be free to become the central rejoicing figure, as the three previously neglected cups are raised in a toast to companionship. Perhaps the previous relationship shown in the two fallen cups was suffocating and dependent, and now the querent has been freed of it by the forces of the Death card, he is free to explore previously hidden or suppressed expressions of his true self, which leads to greater happiness and popularity.

The Death card finds a natural companion in the Empress, as the two sides of the cycle of creation and destruction, but also combines well with many others.

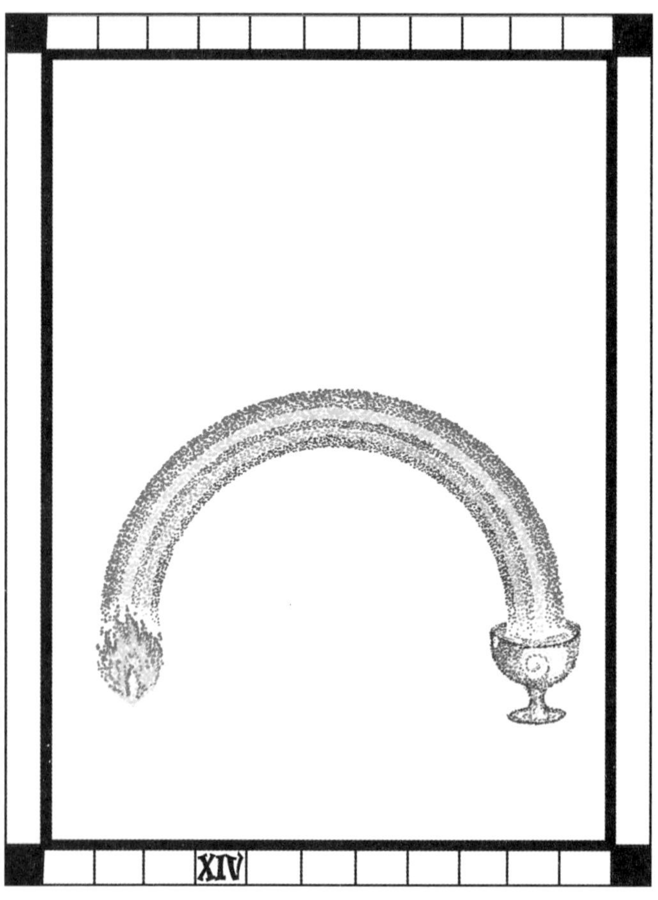
XIV

XIV-Temperance

This is a card that seems to hold many secrets, and can be rather mysterious and difficult to interpret. The traditional image features an angel pouring liquid between two cups, with one foot on land and the other in water. Her serene presence has here been translated into a rainbow, bridging a chalice of water and a flame. The alchemical element of this card is highly significant, and truly understanding the mysteries of alchemy may be more than a lifetime's work. Temperance signifies the alchemical meeting of fire and water, which combine to form steam. It is through the seemingly magical combination of the fiery energy of sunlight with water droplets that produce the spectacular rainbow in which we can behold the full spectrum of seven colors. The layers of symbolism present within this process and the card which represents it are deep and complex and each of us may find new insights from their contemplation and exploration.

Fire as an element represents the creative spirit, the driving energy behind our actions and the divine spark that resides within us all. Without that spark we would be no more than autonomous zombies, but without tempering qualities, this spark could also consume us. Water represents our emotional self, and is the natural opposite and complement to fire. It is also worth noting that although earth is the element normally associated with our physical bodies, water is a more dominant element in our physical makeup. However, with too much water, or, as it symbolizes, too much indulgence in human emotion or the physical realm, the fire of our soul is dampened. The rainbow of Temperance, then, represents the beauty and harmony that may be revealed within us when we can bring our physical and spiritual selves into true balance. Without either the light of our spirit or the drops of our humanity, the full spectrum of our true selves will remain hidden.

Divinatory Meaning

When the rainbow of Temperance appears in a reading, there may be deep processes at work, though on a more mundane level, she has been known to appear as a warning not to drink too much at that party! The message of Temperance is one of control, harmony and balance, the importance of bringing the right ingredients together in just the right quantities. Of course if you've had a hard day at work there is no harm in joining friends for a few drinks, but over indulgence would be counter-productive, not only making you ill and ruining your intended enjoyment, but would have consequential effects on the next day. When reading on earthly matters, Temperance can offer us advice on our health, either as advocation of a new diet plan, or simply recommending that we drink more water. She may also offer us guidance in keeping the right balance between work and family. As always, try to listen to the voice of intuition as you interpret the card, and look at the other cards in the combination for clarification.

On a spiritual level, Temperance speaks of the potential for true communion with our higher selves. Through balance of all aspects of our personality, there is no distraction from the conflicting ego, and the true voice of the higher self, or the 'holy guardian angel' as it is known in ceremonial magick may be heard.

When Temperance is reversed, elements may be dangerously out of balance, and this may result in illness, both mental and physical and a life in chaos. Outside help may be needed to restore this lost balance, as communion with the higher self may have been disrupted.

Here is an example of a three-card combination featuring Temperance:

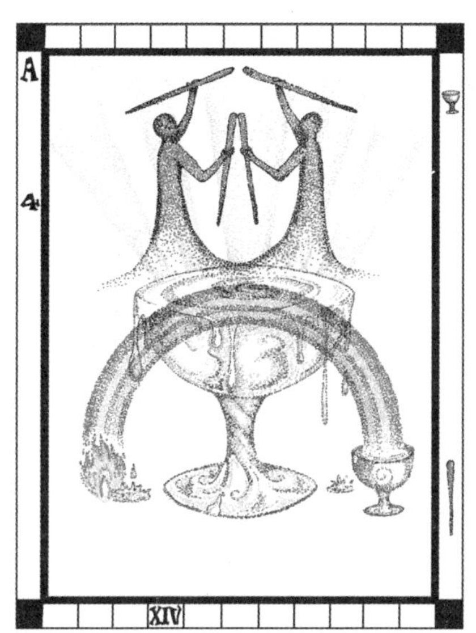

In this combination, the rainbow of Temperance seems to have been formed from the meeting of the fiery Four of Wands and the overflowing Ace of Cups. The two cards of the Minor Arcana seem to compliment the message of Temperance perfectly as everything in this image speaks of harmony, co-operation and integration. The Ace signifies a source of true emotional inspiration, perhaps a new relationship or means of creative expression. The Four of Wands demonstrates the creative dynamic of true partnership, and the ability to lay down strong foundations for future spiritual prosperity. These two elements come together forming a wonderfully balanced and aesthetic image, reflected in Temperance's rainbow arc. In short, partnership with a significant other has made both parties more than the sum of their parts, and all elements of life are coming into a fruitful stability and balance.

Temperance combines well with most cards, most notably the High Priestess, as the cup and flame seem to rest on the pages of her book.

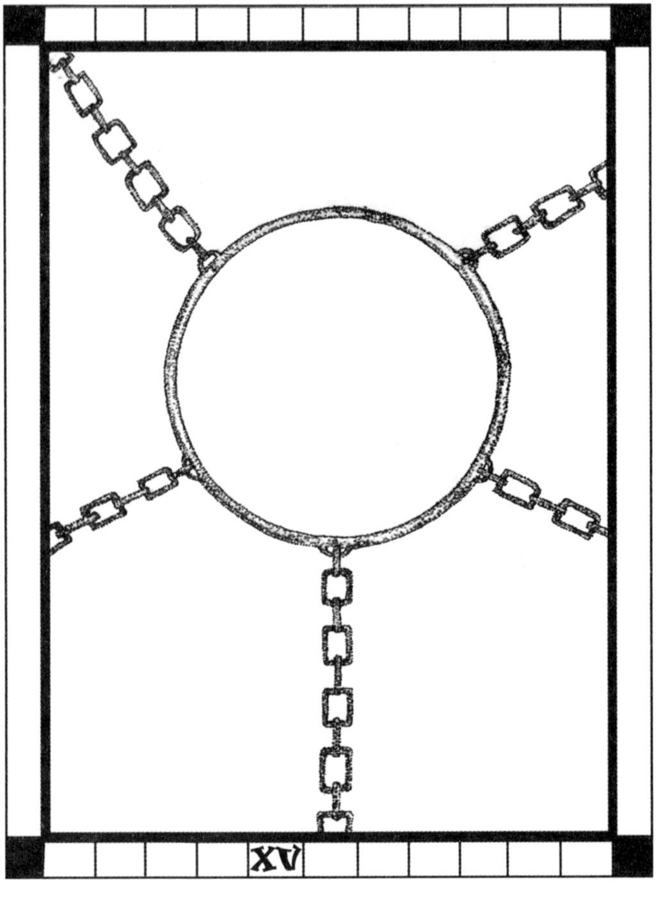

XV-The Devil

The Devil, like Death, is one of those cards that inspire an almost unavoidable negative reaction upon its mere mention, let alone its appearance in a reading. Conventional versions of this card show us a dramatic scene of bondage and indulgence, with a naked male and female connected by loose fitting chains around their necks to a platform on which sits the dominant figure of Baphomet, or the Christian Devil. Traditional versions also tend to feature an inverted pentagram, a shape which I have subtly echoed in my own simplified interpretation.

Of all the seventy-eight cards in the Tarot, this is possibly the most subjective and difficult to define and interpret. To someone of devout Christian faith, there may be a tendency to see this card as a representation of evil in a pure and literal sense, and on a deeper level, the temptations of the flesh. On the other hand, a follower of pagan traditions may see an aspect of their horned god, sometimes known as Cernunnos, and not necessarily see indulgence in the temptations of the flesh as such a bad thing. Hence the traditional meanings which are attached to this card have acquired many subjective and personal additions over the years.

This card is known as 'The Lord of the Gates of Matter'. Essentially this means that it represents the material realm, with all its pleasure and pitfalls. Our relationship with the physical realm is shown by the chains, which is why I chose them as the key symbol for this card. Chains are a temporary addition to our natural state, limiting us and giving us clear boundaries to what we can achieve. If we live our life in invisible chains, we may never realize our full potential. However, once the chains are acknowledged and explored, it may be possible to escape their bonds. So, the Devil may signify dangerous addictions or dependency on material goods, but he also holds the key to overcoming restrictions and taboos and can show the way to freedom from the chains. Some individuals may, however, feel safer within the defined boundaries of their material life. There are many mysteries of self-knowledge that may be explored through the study of this card.

What must be remembered here is that a Tarot card is essentially a key, in the form of a symbol or collection of symbols, designed to unlock your inner wisdom. Therefore it is your personal relationship with this card that will come to define how you interpret it.

Divinatory Meaning

As always, it is important to look at the context of the card within a reading and in relation to the question. The Devil may indicate an addiction or overindulgence in some physical matter, which could be anything from trivial matters like excessive shoe shopping to more life-threatening drug abuse and alcoholism. On a lesser level, he holds a mirror up to our bad habits and patterns of behavior. He can also indicate strong temptations of material indulgence. However, one of the lessons that this card offers is that wisdom is often obtained through living through these experiences rather than avoiding them outright. This is not to suggest that addiction could ever be a good thing, but that indulgence in physical pleasure is not something to be ashamed of, as long as we know and enjoy it for what it is. For some people, the limiting chains are their self denial rather than material attachments. The Devil may indicate a situation in which the querent feels bound or limited in some way, and often feelings of guilt are attached.

Within a combined image, this card tends to add a defined boundary and constriction to the scene and figures that may appear.

When this card appears reversed, then freedom from the chains is being offered. Addictions may be battled successfully, temptations avoided, and habits broken.

Here is an example of a three-card combination featuring the Devil:

In this image we can see the confident Queen of Wands towering over the defeated Five of Swords. The chains of the Devil seem to contain the Queen, and yet the Five of Swords seems free of their confines. One possible interpretation is that perhaps the broken swords of the Five are a broken habit which enables his freedom from the confining chains. As the Queen of Wands is a character with great charisma and self confidence, this may have been a habit or addiction that made the querent feel somehow bigger and more capable. However, as she is almost part of the chains I would suggest that this appearance and feeling was quite superficial. It could be that the Queen of Wands indicates an individual with whom the querent was involved, but that the relationship was unhealthy. This leaves the querent with a feeling of loss, but the freedom from bondage will lead to greater self knowledge and a broadening of horizons.

The Devil is designed to combine particularly well with the Sun and the Moon, as happiness and dreams have their own chains to be uncovered.

XVI

XVI-The Tower

This card, also sometimes known as 'Le Maison Dieu' or 'House of God', takes its title from the traditional image of a Tower which is struck by lightning. Two figures can usually be seen falling from the upper windows, and often a crown can be seen being blasted from the top of the tower by the force of the divine bolt. It is the bolt of lightning itself which I chose to encapsulate the meaning of this card, as the aspects of life normally signified by the structure of the Tower itself may be well represented by the other cards chosen to combine with this image.

Of all the cards, it is the appearance of the Tower which is most likely to perturb the experienced reader. The bolt of lightning of this card represents powerful cosmic forces of unveiling and truth, often accompanied by uncomfortable and sudden change. The power of this card is one of the simplest and clearest to interpret, as it essentially means that nothing will be the same again.

The Tower speaks of forces that tear down all that has been built up, leaving only the foundations behind. It is important, though, to remember that the structure may not have been so sound in the first place, and the opportunity to rebuild in the light of new experience is often a blessing in disguise.

There are similarities here with the Hindu goddess Kali. She also is feared for her destructive nature, but those who know her better know that she is the slayer of demons and the heads she takes are the false masks we wear. Destruction and creation are part of the raw divine power of nature, and it is this force that is found in Kali and the Tower.

It is no coincidence that the lightning shape is echoed in the practice of Qabalah and one of the paths on the Tree of Life. This lightning bolt descends in a flash from the highest point of pure spirit and inspiration, Kether, to the base physical realm, Malkuth. In essence, the lightning is the voice of pure truth from the highest spiritual level, which destroys in a flash all false constructions and many of the comfortable and convenient illusions we may have surrounded ourselves with. The Tower carries a powerful message indeed, and, if it is embraced, can bring a positive and constructive final outcome, once the debris is cleared away.

Divinatory Meaning

There is no doubt that there is a destructive, cleansing element to the Tower, and when it appears in a reading it normally indicates the break down of that which was once familiar. This may mean the abrupt end to a relationship or other situation that seemed stable, but usually when the situation is looked at truthfully and with hindsight, the storm clouds will have been seen on the horizon long before the lightning appeared. Although the change brought by the Tower is often, (but not always), painful and traumatic at the time, the lessons learnt by the experience are invaluable, as is the opportunity to rebuild from the foundations up. On a mundane level, this may be as simple as losing a long-held position at work, but with this card there is always a deeper process underneath the surface. That job may well have been the wrong place for you to be, and the loss of it sets in motion the potential to achieve your true life path.

In a reading on more spiritual or magickal matters, this card can have a very much more welcome and subtle effect. The Tower shows us the way to strip the illusions inherent in physical life away to see the true workings of spirit underneath. This card teaches us a powerful way of unlocking our true spiritual potential.

When the Tower appears reversed, then the truth remains unacknowledged, and the process of change may become more drawn out and painful, possibly even rotting away the essential foundations. Remember, it is better to rip the band-aid off quickly than to tug at it slowly a little at a time!

Here is an example of a three-card combination featuring the Tower:

The Tower strikes at the contented Nine of Cups, whilst nearby, the Four of Pentacles clings tightly to his possessions. There is an interesting dynamic here between the two figures which seems to be the key to this combination. The cups card looks feminine and generous in nature, holding her cup to her heart showing her openness, and the other cups free for others to come and drink from as they wish. She offers happiness and fulfillment

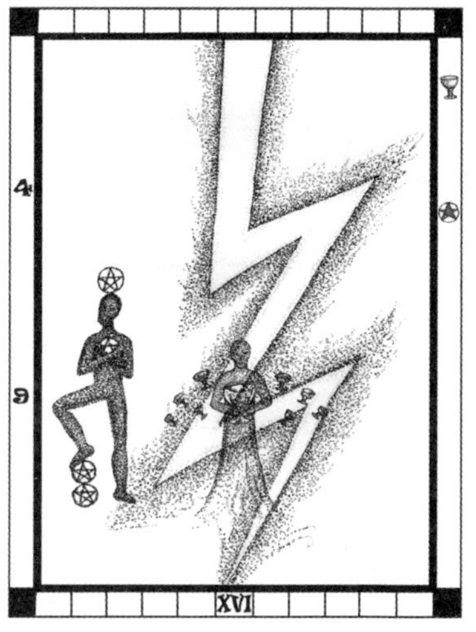

to those who would drink. Conversely, the Four of Pentacles appears masculine and possessive, keeping his disks under guard with an almost arrogant attitude. It seems he would be all too happy to take all that the Nine of Cups has to offer, without giving anything in return. Most likely, this suggests an imbalanced relationship between two individuals, and the influence of the Tower is showing an end to the generous spirit of the Nine. It could be that she has simply had enough of pandering to the needs of the other figure, or that circumstances or even an accident mean that she is either no longer in the picture or is no longer able to offer her kindness. The dynamic of this couple is altered forever, and they must adapt or go their separate ways.

The Tower combines well with all cards, as lightning may strike anyone, and anywhere.

XVII-The Star

The Star is the hope that shines from the void that the lightning of the Tower leaves behind. In most decks, this card can be seen as a clear representation of the zodiacal sign Aquarius, as a young beautiful woman with two urns pours water onto the earth, (or sometimes over herself), and into a still lake, lit by stars. Often the star which dominates the sky is the seven-pointed star, or septagram, and that is my choice here for the key symbol for this card.

The septagram has many correspondences and spiritual assignations. As the Star of Venus, she radiates love, beauty, and compassion, all factors that may be expressed by this card in divination, meditation, or magick. As the Star of Babalon, she speaks of the principles of Thelemic magick—"Love is the law, love under will". The Septagram is also known as the Faerie or Elven star, where the seven points represent the elements and the qualities of the divine uniting with the earthly powers. The seven points may also be seen to represent the seven main chakras, or energy points of the body in balance and harmony. All of these meanings add depth to the essential qualities of this card, which always radiates peace and enlightenment.

The Star reveals the light and beauty of our own inner divinity, the spark that is left behind when all else is stripped away. When the knowledge of this essence is revealed to us, and we have a glimpse of our own soul, there is an inherent knowledge of our eternal nature, and trivial problems melt away. The Star is indeed a guiding light, but it comes as much from within as from above, and the sense of connectedness with spirit and the universe it brings fills the soul with hope, peace and joy.

Divinatory Meaning

Within a reading, the Star will shine her light on all the other cards, raising them to her level. Her message is that there is always hope, no matter how dark things may seem. The darker the night sky, the clearer her light may appear. She will often appear in a reading when there is an opportunity to realize a dream, and is a wonderful indicator of success in any creative project. The Star speaks of self-love, the realization of one's true beauty and nature, which includes sharing that gift with others through music, art and other creative means. She encourages us to shine with our own light and express our divinity in a way that may enable or inspire others to do the same. The Star may indicate a spark of great inspiration and the vision to carry it through into reality, as she is the voice of our muse.

As a person or figure in our lives she may be a highly creative and inspirational individual of great charisma, with a dreamy yet creatively dynamic nature. If not someone who is especially creative herself, she, (or he), may be a figure of great beauty and qualities, both inner and outer, which inspire the creativity of others. The Star may also represent someone whose connection with the divine and compassionate nature makes them an ideal healer or medium.

If this card is negatively aspected in a reading, then the querent's inspiration or connection with higher levels is temporarily clouded or blocked. There may be a feeling of hopelessness and despair. In these times it is important to remember that the light is always there, even if we can't always see it and feel its influence.

Here is an example of a three-card combination featuring the Star:

Here the figure of the Four of Swords rests under the protection of the King of Pentacles, from whom the light of the Star shines brightly. This combination suggests that the querent has been through a challenging and draining time from which to recover. The time has come to rest and recuperate, which in this case means entrusting their care and management of

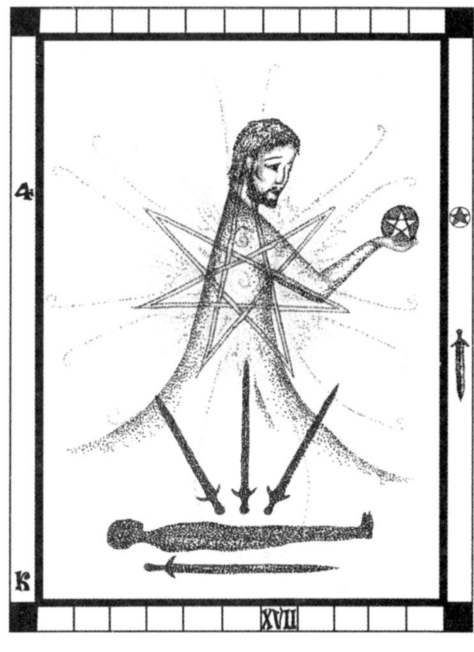

material matter to another. This person is a mature, practical and caring individual, represented by the King. His care will nurture the inner spark, energy, and confidence of the querent. If the querent can allow him to take the weight off their shoulders for a time, then the fire of inspiration and the energy to carry dreams into reality will soon return.

The Star combines particularly well with Judgment, as they are both expressions of inner fire. The Star is the dream, and Judgment is the manifestation.

XVIII

XVIII-The Moon

The Moon of Tarot is at least as enigmatic as her physical counterpart. Debate still rages about the true meaning of the traditional imagery, with a wolf and a dog howling at the central moon, framed by two towers, her light reflected in a pool and stream winding off into the distance. In this card, the hidden knowledge and potential mysteriously hinted at in the new moon of the High Priestess is revealed in full, hence the choice for the full moon as the symbol for this card. The veil is lifted and the gateway stands open, waiting for you to walk through. The eyes of everyday vision are closed, and the third eye awakes, for it is not the everyday world that the Moon invites us to, but the ever-shifting chthonian underworld.

As those familiar with journeying in the otherworld will know, it is a wondrous and inspiring place, but also unnerving at times, and can be dangerous without protection and guidance. For those who do not consciously venture into this realm, it is the land of both dreams and nightmares, and as experience of this land is highly subjective and personal, so it has been with definitions of the Moon. Many see it as a fearful card, many more see it as purely positive. The truth is most likely a little of both, as we get out of this card what we bring to it.

It may be helpful to think of the world as existing in three layers: the upper world, which is the realm of angelic forces, stars, and great teachers and is represented in Tarot by the Star; the middle world which is where we dwell in our physical existence and whose best qualities are seen in the Sun card; and the underworld, the realm of ancestors, magick, faeries, and untold dreams, which we are exploring now, with the Moon card.

The Moon is the layer of shadows and mists that supports and inspires the apparent world. Within this realm are all our hidden truths and lies, and we may see our selves reflected back in a strange mirror. To be able to face and integrate our shadow-self is an empowering and magickal act, but for some it may be most uncomfortable. This is one of the many challenges and blessings that this card offers. The Moon is the invisible force that governs our own cycles of waxing and waning through our lives, and our own inner tides. She shows us many faces, maiden, mother and crone, and hidden aspects of ourselves within them. To be able to encounter these workings and integrate the knowledge of them can lead to great wisdom. Visiting the Moon's realm can bring real gifts of creative inspiration, knowledge and power, but it can also bring madness to those who linger too long. It is a land of whispers and enchanting siren songs, like a night-time forest which can be all too easy to lose oneself in.

Divinatory Meaning

When the Moon appears in a reading, she speaks of things which may be currently unseen, but are no less real for it. She may indicate processes that are in motion behind the scenes which the querent may not yet be aware of, but that will come to impact on their life in some way. The Moon also often indicates events which are cyclic, and may warn someone of being caught in a cycle of repeating events which they must break out of.

Most often though, the Moon speaks of intangible and mysterious events, or even just sensations and feelings. There may be a message trying to reach you through dreams, or from a deceased relative or loved one. It may be a time of increased understanding of life's mysteries, and a deeper exploration of the self. For those who practice magickal or creative arts, this card shows a time of immersion in that magick or creativity. The Moon's appearance often shows a time of increased psychic ability and awareness.

When the Moon is reversed, it seems that the realm of magick and the underworld has become more real than the physical world for a time. The gateway has been passed through and left behind. Though great knowledge and wisdom may be gained by this experience, it will seem like a form of madness, until the gateway back to this reality is found once more.

Here is an example of a three-card combination featuring the Moon:

In this combination it seems that the generous spirit of the Six of Pentacles is near the surface, whilst the sorrow of the Three of Swords is revealed by the Moon's insight. It may be that someone in the querent's life, or the querent himself is looked up to as a philanthropist and friend to the less fortunate. In fact, under the surface, he or she is secretly the one who needs help and support. The Moon offers the opportunity to heal the problem at its source, but this may need the help of a shaman or one who knows their way through the twisting paths of the underworld.

The Moon combines well with the Star, the Sun, and the World, as well as many others.

XIX

XIX-The Sun

The Sun is an expression of accomplishment and pure joy. There is an innocence to this card which is particularly apparent in traditional decks where a naked child rides on the back of a white horse, warmed by the rays of the golden sun. This is the youthful figure of the Greek god Apollo, who is the god of music and poetry and later became associated with the sun god, Helios. For this deck, the image has been simplified to a beneficent and joyful face in the sun itself, radiating amber light. The eyes of the Sun are wide open, as this card deals with the apparent world, (or middle-world), and the physical manifestation of dreams and ambitions.

Inspirations and dreams that may have come from the Star and Moon cards now reach their true expression in the Sun, which bursts forth with abundance and creativity. Long planned projects finally see the light of day, and great success shines its light on all who come under the influence of this card.

There is a feeling of being reborn that comes with this card, like a bright and golden dawn after a long and fraught night. There are no fears and shadows that can escape the all-pervading glow of the Sun, and all phantoms and nightmares are chased away, leaving only the great light.

The light of the Sun reaches so deeply into ourselves that we realize it is also emanating from our souls. As the Star gave us the hope and inspiration of connection with the divine, so the Sun gives us the true realization of the fact. Under the influence of this card, we realize our part of the divine whole, and express it freely, through dance, music, art, or whatever medium suits us best. The seeds that were laid in both the underworld and upper world grow into their full potential under the life-giving light of the Sun.

In many ways, the Sun is one of the simplest cards of the deck. Under the Sun's influence we may experience the world through the eyes of a child, with wonder and joy in our hearts. All is bright, energies are flowing high, and success is assured.

Divinatory Meaning

The Sun's appearance in a reading insures that all neighboring or combined cards will be seen in their most positive light. In career matters, this card may either signify success in an existing job, promotion, or even a new career entirely. In this case, it will be something which truly enables the querent to realize their potential and contribute creatively. Those in creative careers will see their talents rewarded and given the acknowledgement they deserve.

Within relationships, an uncomplicated and guilt-free joy may be found, that involves celebrating each other's gifts and truly basking in the glow of each other's company.

On a spiritual level, it is not a card of challenges and delving deep, but one of the celebration and expression of our own divinity, and true enjoyment of the beauty of the world and its inhabitants.

The Sun may also represent an actual person in the life of the querent, in which case it will be someone of great confidence, with a presence that always seems to light up the room.

In some cases, the light of the Sun may reveal secrets that have been long hidden. While this is positive in the long term, the moment of revelation itself can be jarring and painful.

When reversed, the Sun may indicate an arrogance that comes from realizing one's own divinity, but forgetting the divinity and wonder of others. This can cause clouds to obscure the Sun's promised success, because the joy offered by the rest of the world has become obscured.

Here is an example of a three-card combination featuring the Sun:

In this combination, the Ten of Cups seem to raise a toast to the Sun, which appears as an enormous halo around the head of the struggling Five of Wands. The Sun smiles fondly on the efforts of the Five of Wands as he beats away invisible combatants with his clubs. The sun seems to say that the time for struggling is past now, for success has been achieved. Competitors melt away under the hot rays of sunlight, and the querent may take time to enjoy all he has achieved. The Ten of Cups shows that it is time to relish the company of a significant other, to be grateful for well-earned abundance. It is time for them to relax and allow the light of joy and celebration into their life.

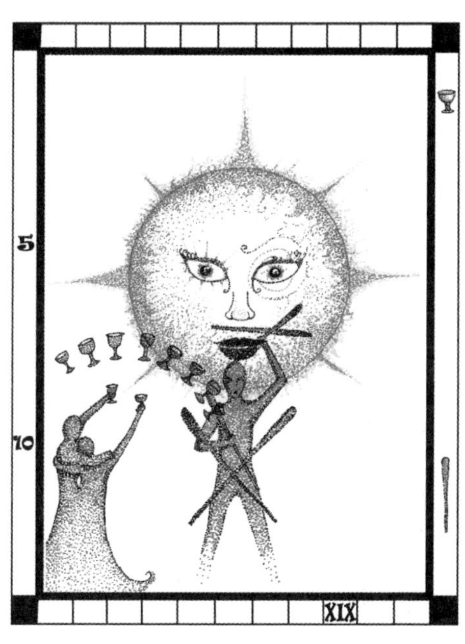

The Sun combines well with many cards.

XX

XX-Judgment

Also sometimes called 'Aeon', the traditional Judgment card features a very biblical looking scene, as a fiery angel wakes the dead with a blast from its trumpet. The message here is one of redemption and rebirth, so the image I have chosen to express this is the phoenix rising from its own ashes. When the phoenix reaches the end of its long life, it builds itself a nest which it then ignites, perishing in the flames. From the ashes of its past form, the glorious phoenix is reborn until the cycle repeats again. Judgment offers us the chance to be reborn like the phoenix, but the past must be assimilated and laid to rest before this transformation can occur.

There are essentially three stages to the process represented by Judgment. Events of the past that have been forgotten or not fully dealt with must be faced and the spiritual lessons, for this is a very spiritual card, must be learned and accepted. Through this process, the spirit is cleansed and may begin anew, with fresh conviction and clarity on the path. Life then ascends to a higher level or vibration, the spirit having evolved beyond its past limitations.

This process may be a daunting prospect for many people, as there is often a tendency to bury and hide away from traumatic events or times when we have acted foolishly or harmfully. There can also be a reluctance to let go of the past and move into a new life. Whilst these aspects remain shamefully locked away and unacknowledged, they can only weigh us down as cause us yet more trouble. When they are analyzed, explored and accounted for, then the past becomes the nest of the phoenix which burns away the old self and allows the new life to emerge.

With this new life comes the confidence to step firmly on your path, whatever it may be, and to be unafraid of the judgment of others. The cards have been laid on the table, and this time there is little doubt that it is a winning hand.

Divinatory Meaning

When Judgment appears in a reading, it indicates a time of reckoning and rebirth. Like an artist who has just completed a great work putting it on display for all to see, it is time for the querent to be seen for who they truly are, warts and all! If the reading is regarding everyday matters, it may refer to a deadline for a major project, or the big performance of a show after weeks of rehearsal. It is time to bring the sum of all that work out into the open, and find its true worth. Before the next level can be reached, the experiences of the past must be assimilated and acknowledged. Like evolution, the next stage is reached by building on what has gone before. Sometimes this may involve facing difficult truths, but acknowledging their value as part of the whole. Once this integration has been achieved, a new chapter opens up in the life of the querent, and they may see their future beckoning.

This sense of moving on to the next level applies to both emotional and spiritual dimensions of this card also. In a relationship, it may indicate an increased honesty between a couple. Perhaps there is something in the past that must be brought out into the open, for good or bad. Once the divulgence is made, it is likely that the partner will accept and respect this new honesty, resulting in deeper levels of trust and intimacy.

If the reading is concerning spiritual or magickal matters, this card gives out a challenge to dig deep and confront anything that could be holding you back from reaching your potential and true divine nature. The process can be harrowing when there are old wounds and ill deeds running deep, but when the challenge is faced, a higher level and vibration may be entered.

If Judgment appears reversed, then the querent may be being haunted and troubled by ghosts from the past, but is unable to bring them out into the open to truly deal with them once and for all. Instead of ascending to a higher level, these old memories pull them down. Like a scene from an old horror movie, the hands of the dead emerge from the grave to try and pull the living down with them. Help may well be needed to combat these inner demons.

Here is an example of a three-card combination featuring Judgment:

Here we see the Eight of Pentacles as he works hard on the final touches to his work. The Page of Swords steps forward bravely, as the phoenix of Judgment flames gloriously into the sky. The Eight of Pentacles is often thought of as the apprentice card. Combined with Judgment, this would be the end of a period of apprenticeship and time to become a master. The work is completed and the time of testing is passed. The Page of Swords is full of youthful enthusiasm and rushes out into the world to share her thoughts and original ideas. All these cards together would seem to speak of a young person graduating with honors and heading rapidly toward a successful career in their chosen field.

Judgment combines well with most cards, particularly the Star and the Sun, which would both be very promising combinations.

XXI

XXI-The World

The World is the end of the journey of the Major Arcana, but what is an end other than the beginning of something new? The traditional image of a figure dancing as the four kerubic beasts watch on has been replaced in this deck by the circle containing a spiral of many colors. The circular shape of this image connects it closely to the Wheel card, but as the Wheel shows the elements and the turning of the year with its clear quarterly divisions, the World brings all things together within one pattern. All the colors of the visible spectrum are represented, to show that all is connected and equal within the World. The circle is a symbol of unity, eternity, and completion, all qualities expressed by this card.

Within the circle is a spiral of all colors. This can be visualized in three dimensions as a gateway through which we may pass. The spiral itself is the most ancient of symbols, reflecting the endless cycle of life, death, and rebirth. It has been scribed by humans in such ancient sites as Newgrange in Ireland, (one of the oldest surviving buildings in the world), and can be found in Nature from the smallest shell to the great spiraling galaxies. Energy moves in spirals, and even our genetic building blocks, D.N.A., takes the form of a spiral pattern.

The World does not speak, then, of just the physical Earth, but rather the whole universe and the interconnectedness of everything and everyone in it. The World gives us a unique view and understanding of the bigger picture, and our place in it. It is this card that links the realms of the underworld, middle world, and upper world together, as represented by the Moon, the Sun, and the Star.

At the end of the journey, we stand back and observe all we have encountered, and reflect on the lessons we have learned. The World shows us that we have achieved much and that it is time at the end, not to stand still and be lost in contemplation, but to celebrate creation, and make ready to start the journey once again.

Divinatory Meaning

When the World appears in a reading, then even the highest goal can be achieved. It is a card which signifies completion and success on a level which impacts positively on the world around you. The World brings a sense of inner wholeness, bringing an individual into holistic balance and an increased awareness of their place in the world.

Ambitions may be realized under the influence of this card, along with respect and support from the outside world. There is a sense of talent being shared and given the acknowledgment it deserves. With this influence, it is a card that may appear when someone is ready to pass their knowledge and skill onto others, as a teacher or mentor, particularly if it appears in combination with the Hierophant.

In relationship or family matters, it shows that there is harmony and wholeness within the couple or family, all the individual ingredients coming together to form a strong, united whole.

Within a spiritual context, the World indicates a great step forward in the achieving of enlightenment, and a greater unity with the higher self. Potential that was glimpsed earlier has been reached. The spirit has learned and assimilated much on its journey and can move on to the next stage. There is no end to this spiritual evolution, for its potential is as infinite as the universe itself, but the same paths crossed again with new eyes bring fresh learning and deeper understanding.

When reversed, this card may indicate frustration in the completion of a task or project. On a deeper level, the deep connection which the World indicates may be temporarily blocked, bringing with it a sense of isolation and limited vision.

Here is an example of a three-card combination featuring The World:

The anxious figure of the Nine of Swords seems to be swept into the spiral of the World, while the Three of Pentacles displays his achievement proudly. These three cards come together to give a picture of someone who has been under a great deal of mental pressure. They have had their goal in sight, but have been worried about their own ability, whether the task was even possible, and how it would be thought of by others. These wor-

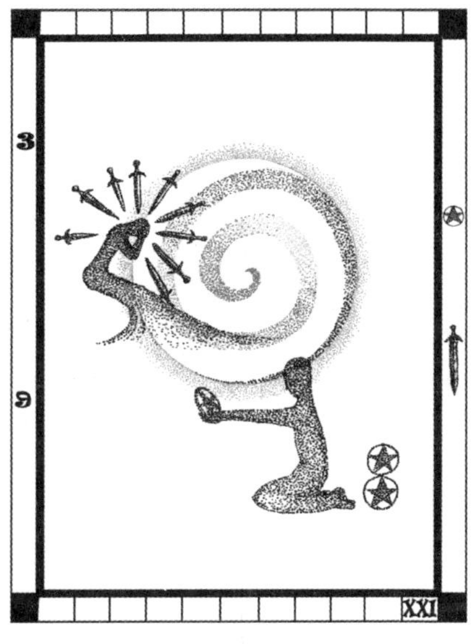

ries are all expressed in the Nine of Swords. The World seems to comfort the despairing figure and take it into itself while the Three of Pentacles observes and shares the completed work. The task is achieved with flying colors, and all success and admiration is due to the querent. The worries will become a part of the past, but have been learned from and integrated into the querent's experience, becoming a welcome part of the new, more confident whole.

The World combines well with the Fool, as the other end of the journey, and also the Star, the Moon, and the Sun as the worlds combined within the greater universe.

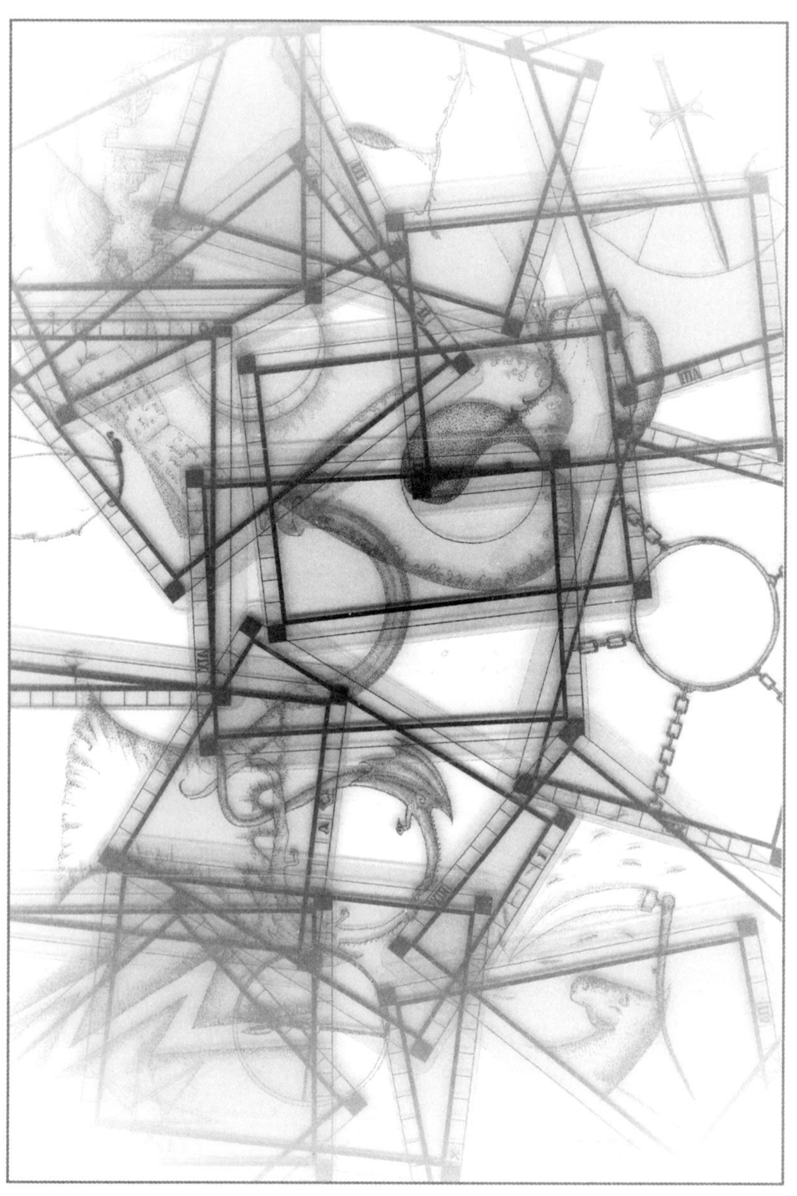

THE MINOR ARCANA

The remaining fifty-six cards of the Tarot are referred to as the Minor Arcana, but the word 'minor' should not be read as meaning that they are any less important. To use a theatrical analogy, if the Major Arcana are the settings and themes of the play, then the Minor Arcana are the characters, motivations, and events—certainly significant! What an unengaging play it would be without them.

Traditionally the Minor Arcana are either pip cards, (sometimes very simple and not entirely unlike playing cards), or scenes in which we see people in various situations from which we determine the meanings of the cards. In *The Transparent Tarot*, the images of the Minor Arcana have been simplified to featureless androgynous figures, in the color of their suit, in very simple but evocative scenes and positions. Again this is to enable any of the cards to combine with each other without confusion, creating images which are very open to intuitive interpretation. The Aces have been given special treatment, as they represent each elemental force in a state of raw potential. Therefore, they are not scenes, but iconic portrayals of each suit's emblem. The Minor Arcana also includes the court cards, which are so different, that they have their own section, following this one.

The Minor Arcana represent the everyday workings of our lives, and are divided into four suits; Wands, Cups, Swords and Pentacles. These suits correspond to the four elements which in turn correspond with forces which are at work in our day to day life.

Wands are red, and aligned with the element of fire. They show what drives us, our energy, passion and strength of will.

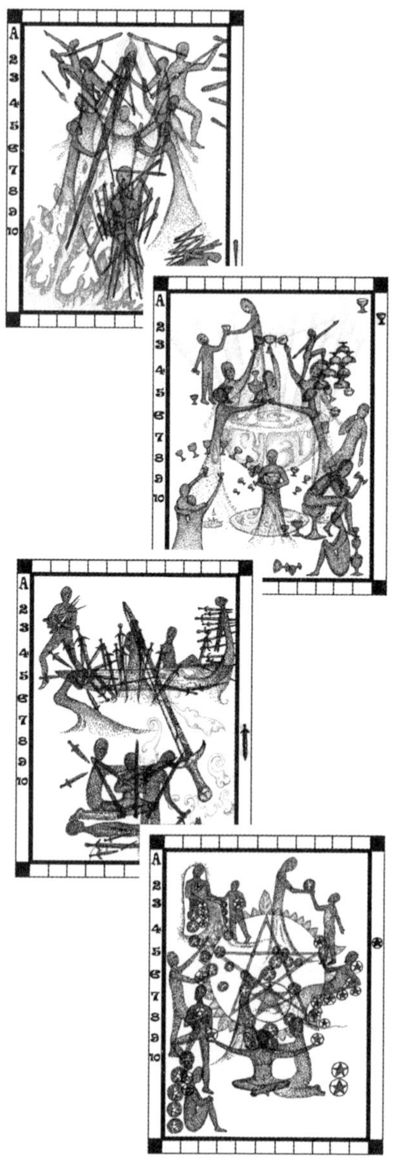

Cups are blue and aligned with the element of water. They show what moves us, and speak of deep emotions and intuition.

Swords are dark purple and aligned with the element of air. They show us the realm of the intellect, logic, and ideas.

Finally Pentacles are green, and aligned with the element of earth. They show us the physical realm, and speak of matters of health, work and finances.

Although these are the prime areas the cards of each suit are concerned with, there are many interpretations for each card depending on the context of the reading, so I have provided suggestions for interpretations on many different levels.

Like the Major Arcana, each suit of the Minor Arcana takes us on a journey. By noting what qualities the preceding and following cards in the sequence might have, and by seeing all the cards of the same number together, we may learn to interpret each one within a wider context. When reading or studying the cards, try asking these questions:

> Regardless of what the book suggests, what is MY first impression of what is happening in this card?
>
> What do I think might have happened just before?
>
> What do I think will happen next?
>
> What are my feelings towards the figure in the card? (i.e. sympathetic, envious, frustrated, proud, loving…)
>
> Does this image resonate with any event or person in my life?
>
> What do I think may be happening beyond the scene on the card?
>
> What smells/tastes/sounds do I associate with this card?
>
> How does this card interact with others in a combination? (i.e. Does it seem dominant or passive? Awkward or well balanced? What might this mean?)
>
> How does this image change when reversed or flipped?
>
> If the figure/s in this card could speak, what would they say?

You may wish to add your own questions and other observations to this list as you work with the cards. Remember to never stop questioning!

The Aces

The Aces are far, far more than just the first of each of the four suits of the Minor Arcana. They are the raw essence of each element, the whole as it appears before it is fragmented to form the rest of the small cards. Whereas the other cards of the Minor Arcana can be directly related to everyday matters and people, the Aces are broader and more difficult to pin down in meaning, as they represent the tendencies, or forces behind the actions of the other cards. The Aces are the elemental powers in their purest and most powerful form, and so can be seen as the seed or root of their relative suit. As their meaning in a reading will be heavily influenced by the cards with which they are combined or which appear around them, so the intense form of their unpolluted energy will give a feel for the nature of the whole reading.

The Aces can also appear as forces in potential, energies which are on the verge of manifesting in the apparent world but have not yet appeared in any form more tangible than a strong sensation. For instance, the Ace of Wands may be the drive and energy needed to begin a new creative project, or the Ace of Cups may be the first stirrings of a love affair.

The four Aces have correspondences not only with the elements, but with the four directions and the seasons. For those who wish to dig deeper into their symbolism, they have correspondences within many esoteric systems, such as the four-part soul structure of Qaballistic belief, as well as in the hallows of ancient Celtic grail lore.

The Ace of Wands

Wands represent the element of fire, and the fiery nature of the Ace of Wands is immediately apparent upon seeing the card, as the wand bursts forth from its ruling element. Fire is the driving force behind all creative and dynamic action, so the Ace of Wands encapsulates that force in its purest form. It is the power of spirit, the spark that dwells within each one of us and shines from within us when we are at our best. Within the Ace of Wands can be found not only great creative and spiritual inspiration, but also the energy needed to act on it.

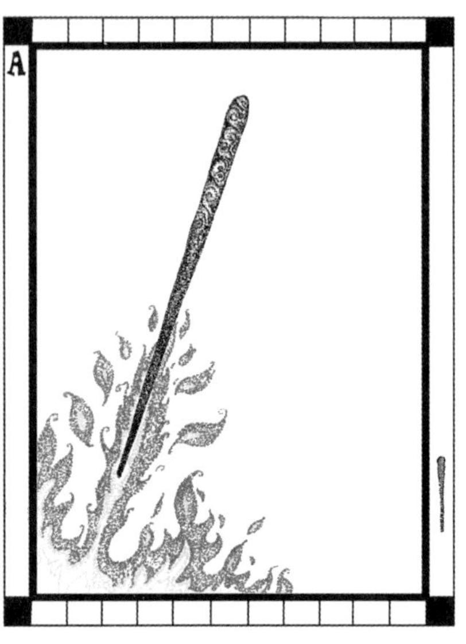

It would take a great naivety to not also notice the phallic nature of this card, and there are certainly connections with male fertility and sex drive, as well as the male aspects of divinity. This card is also associated with the season of summer, the sun, and , (for those in the Northern Hemisphere), the direction of south.

Because the Ace of Wands is the purest form of these energies, it tends to have a positive meaning and effect on any reading or combination in which it appears.

Divinatory Meaning

When the Ace of Wands appears in a reading, it signifies a time of great potency. Creative ideas may be surfacing with great momentum, and life seems to be bursting forth with new found vigour. When seeking guidance in career issues, it is a sign which may herald a positive start to any new project or enterprise, or a renewed freshness of enthusiasm and drive within an existing career. It is a card which is far more about creative satisfaction and fulfilment than it is about financial security, but that does not mean that it will lack that dimension. Because of the charisma and potential energy tied up with this card, material rewards will likely emerge in time and of their own accord, without being overtly sought.

Within a relationship, this is most definitely the card of lust and sexual chemistry. In this case, it would be important to look at the other cards in the combination to see if emotional compatibility is present, if indeed it is sought. One thing that is certain with this card is that there would be no lack of interest or ability in the bedroom! However, it may lack the stability for a long-term relationship, or its nature may change with time.

The Ace of Wands is also a promising card when related to spiritual or magickal matters, indicating a renewed divine energy on which to draw, and the ability to manifest intent and desire. In this area it particularly relates to Yang energy, and the masculine proactive urge.

When negatively aspected, however, the fiery energies of this card may be dampened or blocked. It may indicate impotency, both metaphysical and literally. Most dangerously, these energies may even be burning out of control, and need to be tempered.

The Ace of Cups

Cups are water, and the Ace is the direct female counterpart to the very masculine energies of the Ace of Wands. The curved and receptive chalice overflows with its element, its purity causing it to glow with a divine light. Here we see a vision of the Holy Grail, showing us the purest qualities of the element of water and the feminine aspects of divinity. Water is the element most closely associated with the emotions and the more intuitive, nurturing, and healing qualities of spirit. The Ace

shows water in its most unpolluted form, and it represents the potential for great depth of love, faith, and a great capacity for hope in any situation. As the Grail, the Ace contains great potential for healing and wisdom.

With only a little imagination, the cup may be seen to resemble a woman's womb, and as such, it represents female fertility and maternal urges. This card also stands for the season of autumn, the moon, and the direction of west.

The pure and untainted nature of this card will usually bring a sense of hope and a depth of feeling to any reading or combination.

Divinatory Meaning

The Ace of Cups stands for new emotions, increased wisdom and the potential for healing within a situation. When reading on a matter of career or finances, this may seem to be an odd card to surface, but it is a good sign that whatever line of work you are in, it has greater depth and significance than just any old job done for the money. There may be an opportunity to work within the community, or to help charitable causes. It may be that some aspect of the career will help you unlock your own depth of feeling and intuition, or set you on the path to healing, either yourself or others. Perhaps an unexpected emotional connection may start to emerge with a work colleague.

If the main issue of the reading is relationships, then the Ace of Cups is a sign that either a potentially deep and rewarding relationship is emerging, or that new layers of expression and empathy are being uncovered in an existing relationship. This may also speak of great friendships, not necessarily always romantic matters.

On a spiritual level, a gateway has been opened to the intuition and a fresh and holistic understanding of the mysteries of the universe is being accessed. It is a time for contemplation and intuition rather than action, and may indicate potential healing abilities coming to the fore. Depending on the surrounding or combined cards, the need for healing may also be indicated.

When the card is reversed, the chalice is overturned. The waters flow out of control often indicating a period of emotional unrest and even illness. Intuition may be misguided, and emotions are so powerful that they become impossible to manage. Eventually the chalice may run dry, leaving an emptiness which is difficult to fill.

The Ace of Swords

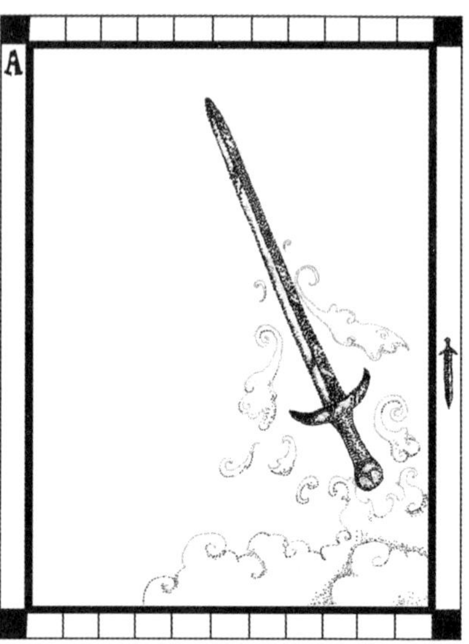

The Ace of Swords represents the potential contained within the element of air, and the mental and rational realm. The sword cuts through the clouds, showing the power of analytical thought and logic to cut through lies and illusion. The potential for original thinking and fast, efficient communication of ideas is contained within this card. The sword is an appropriate symbol to portray 'sharp' thinking, but its double-edged nature reminds us that the power of the mind can be as destructive as it is creative. The creative nature of this Ace is the power to bring thoughts and ideas into reality, unmarred by foggy thinking or obstacles of practicality. This card also stands for academic achievement and new learning, particularly in the area of science.

The Ace of Swords can be compared to King Arthur's famed sword, Excalibur, which shone as a symbol of justice and unity. However, when it was used for selfish purposes, the blade shattered. So may it be with the qualities of this Ace—if the motives remain pure, then success is assured, but the mind itself will suffer if the energies of this card are used for ill purpose.

The Ace of Swords is aligned with the season of spring and the direction of East. Just as the sun rises in the east, so the Ace of Swords brings the light of knowledge and intellectual insight to any reading.

Divinatory Meaning

Within any reading, the Ace of Swords will bring a sense of clarity and truth. Ideas in any area of life which once seemed confusing and complicated may now start to make sense. Within material or career matters, this card signifies the birth of a fresh and innovative idea, perhaps for a new business, or a new way of working. This card may well signify new and highly useful developments in technology. Communication between colleagues will be clear, and sharp thinking will start to bring tangible results. Ideas which may once have seemed unachievable will now start to find ways to manifest. If it is a matter of money that the reading is concerned with, look to any fresh and original ideas that seem to present themselves, for they will most likely be successful.

In matters of the heart, the Ace of Swords is an indicator of a relationship emerging between intellectual equals who may enjoy a healthy debate! This card is a good sign that there are no hidden secrets waiting to be uncovered, and no mixed signs. The sort of relationship shown by this card makes rational and logical sense, but may not be overtly passionate or emotional. However it could indicate an improvement of honest communication between a couple.

Magickal or spiritual developments indicated by this card may be an increased interest and understanding in complex systems such as the Qaballah, Enochian Magick, or other complex ritual paths. It is a card of great emerging intellectual comprehension as opposed to intuitive or practical understanding. However, it may signify a moment of great insight on any path, even increased control of dreams and accuracy of predictions in divination.

When the Ace of Swords is reversed, however, it is a sign of false insights and deluded thinking. The mind may not be functioning as it should, and can create illusion and paranoia, as can be seen manifested in many of the later Swords cards.

The Ace of Pentacles

As can easily be discerned from the above image, the suit of Pentacles is aligned with the element of earth, and the Ace of Pentacles represents all the potential of that element in its purest form. Matters of physical health and material stability are ruled over by this suit, with the Ace promising the beginnings of tangible achievement in these matters. The symbol of the pentacle within a circle is suggestive of wholeness and balance, and certainly it is a card which implies good health and a solid foundation.

All the Aces have an intrinsically creative nature, as they are potential in an emerging form. The creative nature of the Ace of Pentacles lies in the realm of nature, and things that grow. It is a creativity of an intensely practical nature, which finds beauty in usefulness. As with the world of nature, it has more of a quality of patience than the other Aces, giving new developments the time they need to develop and mature naturally.

The Ace of Pentacles, along with the rest of its suit, also represents the season of winter, and the direction north.

The material nature of the Ace of Pentacles is not yet tainted with greed or indulgence as it stands for this element in its purest form.

Divinatory Meaning

The Ace of Pentacles is almost always a positive influence and an excellent sign of success and future prosperity within a reading or combination. It may indicate a new and potentially profitable career, or at least positive financial developments within an existing job. Certainly if new material stability is sought, then this Ace is a great indicator that it may be achieved. On a physical level still, this card is also an excellent sign of emerging good health, perhaps in the form of a new, (and not intolerable), diet or exercise regime. This card speaks of a holistic and balanced approach to health, with all the body's needs met naturally.

For a potential or existing relationship, the Ace of Pentacles shows a down to earth, no-nonsense sort of romantic partnership, which is perfect for people who don't wish to get carried away by lust, emotional tides, or intellectual discussion. That's not to say that this sort of relationship can't be passionate, for there is much enjoyment of physical pleasures to be found in this card. The difference is that the essence of a relationship represented by the Ace of Pentacles has a far more stable and rooted nature than can perhaps be seen in the others, which may be the grounding that a strong romantic relationship needs in order to last and bear fruit—depending always, of course, on other combined or surrounding cards.

If the reading is regarding magickal or spiritual matters, the Ace of Pentacles may symbolise a developing skill in nature magick, traditional witchcraft, or possibly herb lore. This card may indicate a potential initiation into Druidry, Shamanism, or Wicca, and certainly an increased awareness of Earth mysteries and care for the planet's welfare.

When this card appears negatively aspected, the need for money and material gain may have overwhelmed other aspects of life in a destructive way. Likewise it can also indicate the development of habits which are harmful to health or the environment.

The Twos

The Twos represent the first stages of manifestation of the potential forces contained within the Aces. As it manifests, the energy of each Ace splits in two, and this set of cards tells the story of how each suit reacts when faced with a duplicate of itself. The dual nature of the Twos can therefore indicate partnerships, conflicts or choices, depending on the nature of the suit, and the environment of the reading. The Twos usually, though not always, represent an early stage of unfolding events, and the energies still have a young feel about them. Therefore, though they have lost the untainted purity of the Aces, they still express a high level of conviction of purpose.

As with all the small cards, the images are simple yet evocative, leaving interpretation very open to intuition. The following are some suggested meanings and possible ways of looking at the cards.

The Two of Wands

This image shows two dynamic figures facing each other in a mirrored pose. Their stance is strong and confident, and each seems the match for the other. They each hold their wand out, so that the two are almost touching.

There are many different ways to view this card, and its meaning may shift from reading to reading according to how the reader perceives the scene. To look at the card from within, that is the perspective of one or both of the figures, we see a meeting of equals. The question is, how will these equals react to each other? The wands are not held in an overtly threatening or aggressive way, but it does not take a great stretch of imagination to picture this scene resolving in conflict. Wands are a fiery energy, and fire may be creative or destructive. Another possibility here is that the figures are indulging in a peacock-like display of new-found power. There is certainly an aspect to this card which speaks of empowerment and the first stages of meeting one's potential. A more peaceful interpretation is that through displaying their power to each other, they may appreciate the other's display and form a dynamic partnership. The realisation that teamwork would make them doubly powerful and productive is certainly a strong possibility in this card.

From the perspective of an observer of the figures, rather than from inside the scene, this card may indicate a choice. Two powerful

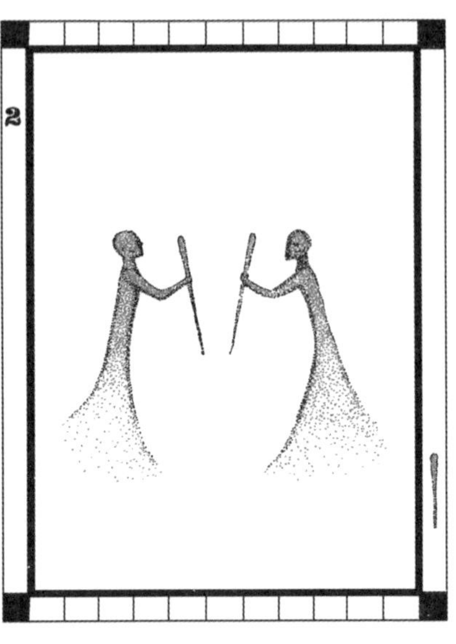

and attractive options are being offered, leading to a diverging path. Almost a form of initiation, one wand must be chosen and its power claimed.

Divinatory Meaning

This card may indicate exciting times and an invigorating energy within a reading. The figures of the Two of Wands are large and centrally placed, so these energies are likely to be quite dominant in a combination.

If the reading is on a career issue, then it may indicate a fruitful yet fiery creative partnership. Within such a partnership inspiration runs high, but both parties have strong ideas and charisma, so may occasionally come into conflict. However there is mutual respect there which keeps the partnership productive, and in fact the odd flaming debate well may be the fuel for great creativity. When not indicating a partnership, it is a time of decision making. Perhaps two equally appealing career paths are on offer, and one must be chosen over the other. The right choice will most likely be made, for this is a card of personal empowerment and discovery.

In health matters there is an emerging drive to get fit, possibly as the result of healthy competitiveness. The energy is certainly present to achieve any health goals, and these are most likely centred around dynamic sports and exercise.

Again, in a relationship, this card may indicate two tempestuous yet artistic personalities who are extremely attracted to each other, and yet often argue. It would be important to look to the other cards to see if the stabilising ingredients are present to make it last, but it would certainly be a passionate and absorbing affair.

In spiritual matters this card may indicate a time of initiation, emerging power, and path choosing. The wands held by the figures represent their personal power, and also seem to form a gateway. It is time to come into your power and pass through the gateway, integrating the energy of the wands into the greater whole.

When reversed, the negative qualities of this card will be highlighted, and it may well indicate arguments and personality clashes, as well as loss of personal power.

The Two of Cups

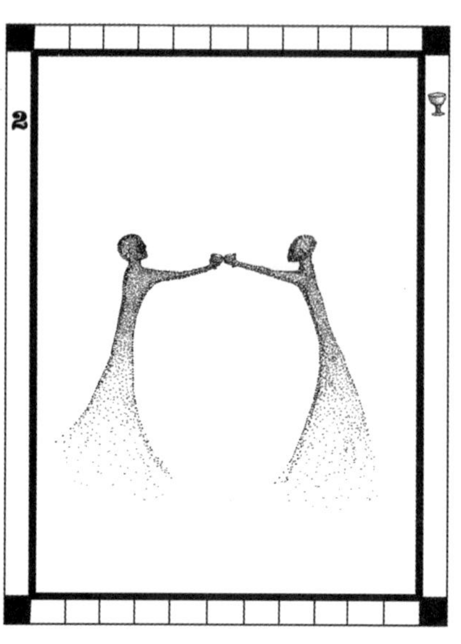

The figures of the Two of Cups face each other in a similar pose to the Two of Wands, but the energy dynamic is very different. One noticeable difference is that the figures actually make contact with each other, their cups meeting in the centre as if in a toast to each other. Although there is still an element of dualism here, as in all the Twos, the couple here is drawn together in peace, reflecting their watery nature. Whereas with the fiery wands there was a magnetic force which could as easily divide as it could attract, here the waters flow together harmoniously. The gentle and intuitive nature of the suit of Cups manifests here as two separate beings who are able to sense and acknowledge their common source. When waters do meet and flow together, they mingle perfectly and become inseparable. Though each flow of water may have had its own qualities, those qualities mingle naturally and with ease. It is as if the raw energy of the Ace of Cups has split, but that the emerging energies remember being one and recognise it in each other. The figures seem to see a reflection of themselves in the other, and that results in an instant understanding and empathy. This can be seen as the card of the soul mates, which has many different levels of meaning within a reading or combination.

Divinatory Meaning

The Two of Cups is likely to bring a harmonious and peaceful energy to a reading. Such an emotional card may not seem appropriate as a good omen in career matters, but it may have many positive implications, even on a material level. The Two of Cups could well indicate a work environment which suits the querent perfectly. In this case, the two figures could represent the mutual benefit found by being exactly the right person for the job. Just as soul mates are such because they are exactly what each other need, so it may be that the querent finds a placement that suits them so perfectly that they are able to be themselves and bring forward all their best qualities, just like in a healthy relationship.

It almost goes without saying that this is a wonderful card to appear in a reading concerning the nature of a relationship. True emotional harmony and a real sense of connectedness may be achieved. This card often appears to signify soul mates, and this may be in friendship as well as romance. Indeed the kind of romance signified by this card has its roots in strong friendship and similar ideals, as opposed to physical attraction. Of course physical attraction may also be present, but it is the spiritual and emotional connection that will have brought them together. The Two of Cups does not always signify the early stages of such a relationship, as it can be a longstanding couple who still have the same feelings between them as when their love was new.

On a spiritual level, this card signifies a partner who can not only understand and support a magickal or spiritual path, but most likely shares the beliefs of the querent. Here are true soul mates who may walk the path together as equals, and who have been brought together to further each other's spiritual development.

If the card appears reversed, it could well be that an obstacle has been placed in the way of the soul mates and for some reason they find it hard to be together at this time. Sometimes two people can know each other too well, and the relationship becomes stale.

The Two of Swords

A figure sits cross legged and blindfolded, crossing two swords in front of himself, which point in opposing directions. As swords represent the element of air and concerned with the workings of the mind, so it is that in the Two of Swords we see the result of opposing ideas emerging and attempting to find a way to be resolved. Unlike the Two of Cups and the Two of Wands, we only see one figure here, balancing the dual forces within himself. That is not to say that the two swords may not represent two people, but

that the key figure is the one who tries to bring them together in harmony. The blindfold suggests impartiality, and also a need to look within for the answers. It is also reminiscent of the traditional portrayal of Justice, and similar ideas of balance and fairness may be evoked. The two swords are pointing harmlessly away from the body and although indicating different directions are not in direct conflict. The position seems for the moment to be stable, although there may be a feeling of being stuck in stalemate. There is also a protective aspect to the figure's pose, both arms and legs crossed, as though there is potential friction which is undesired and is being staved off. This same protective pose, with the arms crossed over the vulnerable heart, also prevents the figure from expressing itself freely. It is very much a fixed and unshifting pose, but not one that can be held comfortably indefinitely. Although this card is in a state of temporary peace, the two opposite ideals cannot be maintained in balance for long, and a choice must be made on which direction is right for now. When the decision is made, the balance will shift and events will start to move forward again, for good or ill.

Divinatory Meaning

When the Two of Swords appears in a reading, it most likely signifies an atmosphere of temporary truce. Two ideologies are attempting to co-exist, and for the moment they are being held in balance, perhaps with the help of a neutral peacekeeper. In the workplace this can manifest as a feeling of tension which has not yet come to conflict, where two equals or two groups within the whole start to see things in very different ways. Though for now it is agreed to disagree, the swords are still upright and ready to fight. For events to move forward, one path must be chosen, which means either one side will be convinced by intellectual discussion to join the other, or they will fight it out amongst themselves. In many ways, then, the two presented paths may also be seen to represent the choice between peaceful resolution and conflict. Perhaps, in the end, the two groups will splinter off by mutual consent, each pursuing their own direction. This may be a group deciding to form a new company of their own in order to explore new directions.

Within a relationship this card may show that a couple have conflicting ideas and aims in life, but have compromised in order to keep the peace. However, if they are to continue together in the long term, one direction must be chosen, otherwise things may grow bitter between them. In the realm of air, there must always be movement, else the situation may become suffocating and oppressive.

In terms of the spiritual life of the querent, the gateway nature of this card becomes very important again. The Two of Swords may indicate someone who keeps the peace but at their own expense. Though peace itself is rewarding, it is difficult to tread two paths at once and give them full energy and commitment. The time may come soon when one path must be chosen over the other, at least for a time, in order to progress.

When this card is reversed, the swords are heavy and cannot be held in balance any longer. Two ideologies may well be about to do battle, with no peacekeeper between them.

The Two of Pentacles

As in the Two of Swords, we see one figure balancing two objects, but here the pose is far more open and less protective. Relating to the element of earth, the Two of Pentacles speaks of material concerns and matters of the physical plane, including health issues. Because it is a single figure as opposed to two, it is attitude of the querent within him or herself which is most likely to be indicated rather than as part of a team or couple. There is a strong sense of self-sufficiency and confidence portrayed by this card. The figure seems to have a more carefree attitude than the preceding Two of Swords, and appears to be balancing the two pentacles with ease. The pentacles themselves may symbolise separate physical demands on the figure, which he seems to be having no problem balancing. Indeed, it looks as if the figure could even consider juggling them!

Another perception of the figure could be that balancing the pentacles is a form of meditation. Certainly he does not appear to be worried or anxious about his responsibilities, and his cross legged and open armed stance is very reminiscent of some traditional meditation postures. It is a special skill that the Two of Pentacles displays, for we cannot always so easily balance or juggle the many aspects of our life!

Divinatory Meaning

Although the Two of Pentacles may indicate someone under the pressure of many roles or tasks, it is a positive indicator that not only will the tasks be dealt with, but that they will be tackled with ease. In fact, the person signified by the Two of Pentacles most likely relishes the challenge and enjoys every minute of it! In a work or domestic situation, this card speaks of a period of multi-tasking. One image may be of someone who manages to not only hold down a successful career, but is a wonderful mother as well! It could appear when someone is doing two jobs at once, with no drop in standards, or two creative projects. However, it is a difficult situation to maintain for long periods. Health-wise, this card is an indicator of a person who is working hard to achieve and maintain balanced health, through both diet and exercise.

If positively aspected within a relationship, it could show someone who is able to dedicate time to their loved one despite having a busy career. However, beware if surrounding or combined cards might show that it is multiple love affairs that are being juggled.

In spiritual matters the Two of Pentacles may show that despite being busy, time can still be found to keep up spiritual practices, but care should be taken that mundane tasks do not overwhelm spiritual needs.

When this card is negatively aspected, the multi-tasking becomes fraught and stressful, and potentially one or both pentacles will be dropped. The time has come to be more selective about tasks, or seek assistance in order to manage them.

The Threes

In the Threes we see the result of the choices made by the Twos. The decision as to what form the potential energy of the Aces would take has now moved on and is showing tangible results. Another way to think about it is that the seed of the Aces was fertilized in the Twos, and now a child grows in the womb.

This child is very much the fruits of its parents' labours—that is, it reflects in a more concrete form the desires or traits of the preceding cards in the sequence. If the Two was a partnership, then the Three shows the results of that partnership. If the Two of the suit signified conflict or choice, then the Three represents the consequences of that conflict or choice. Again, each suit's reaction to these factors is affected according to the nature of the element they represent.

The Three of Wands

The tension and potential of the Two of Wands has resolved itself successfully. After having discovered the potential power of teamwork, the results begin to show. In the Three of Wands we can now see three figures; two which seem to mirror each other, still reminiscent of a gateway, and a third between them. The gateway of initiation has been passed through, and the time of testing is over. In this card, the three wands come together at their tips, and the fire of creation is formed where they meet. Not only do the three wands touch, but the three figures themselves seem joined together, indicating that the individuals have formed a strong unit. Three is a powerful and balanced number, and a creative team forged on this energy has the ability to thrive. The flame seen here is the first spark of success. Any conflicts have been settled not only peacefully and productively, and individual drives and talents have come together to form something greater than the sum of their parts. There is a sense of great hope in this image, as if there are greater things yet to come.

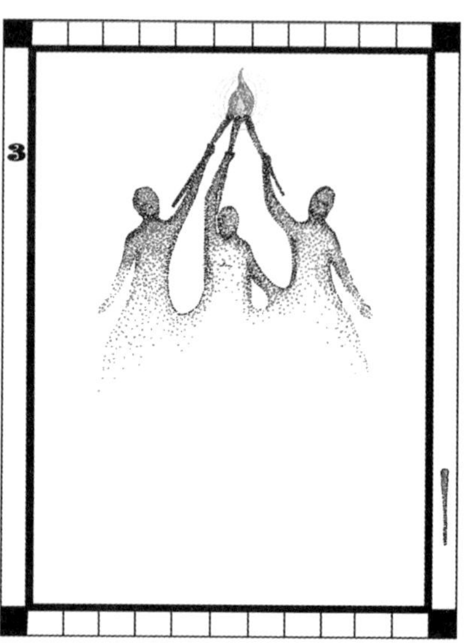

Divinatory Meaning

The Three of Wands is full of wonder, creativity, and enthusiasm. A project in its early stages starts to come together with very positive results which could lead to a bright future for all concerned. This card may come up when a new band play their first successful gig, the efforts each member has put into their individual roles paying off and creating a powerful end result. In a work situation, this card shows that the right people or the right ingredients have been put in place, and the rewards are starting to show.

Within more romantic concerns, a relationship that began as a fling may develop into something more profound. Common interests and aims may be discovered, and activities that can be enjoyed together may even lead to creative enterprises. This is a couple who are good for each other, and create an exciting atmosphere in a group.

The Three of Wands is also a promising card to appear in a reading concerning spiritual or magickal matters. Real results are starting to be seen after the discovery of hidden power. It could be a sign of a group working together and starting to see just how effective their work can be. When these first results start to show, it is important to maintain humility and respect for the entire group, for increase of power can often dissolve a unit from within, or even explode it dramatically if not properly grounded!

When reversed, the situation may not be a stable as could be wished. There is a danger here when the first successes occur that an individual or even a group can become arrogant and overly proud. It is also important to be sure that this new-found power is not be misused or directed at others in a destructive way.

The Three of Cups

The couple of the Two of Cups have been joined by a third figure, and spirits appear to be high. Love has flourished and multiplied, giving the Three of Cups good cause for celebration. Whereas the Two of Cups showed the spark of recognition between soul mates, the Three of Cups shows familiarity, friendship and fun! True friendship is a great gift, and this card, though it may signify many things, shows that friendship itself is justification for rejoicing. Again, as in the Three of Wands, the

three figures seem to be joined together, here indicating their common natures and acknowledgement of spiritual connectedness. The stable nature of the Three means that the connection between these friends runs deeply and will last through difficulties as well as the good times indicated here. Their cups are raised high, the drinks overflowing with joy. Whether they are toasting a birth, a marriage, or simply each other, one thing is certain; it's going to be a party to remember!

Divinatory Meaning

The Three of Cups is always a welcome sign in any reading. In whatever context this card appears, it generally means a celebration of some sort is in order. In a work situation this could be a big office party where people are able to let their hair down and show their true colors, or it may be toasting the success of a recent project or venture. A great sense of camaraderie may be felt, and the work environment spoken about by this card would certainly be a friendly and productive one.

This card may also signify a get together among good friends, or a family who is happy and thriving. Engagement parties, christenings, bah mitzvahs, and birthdays are all events that could be represented by this card. The key points here are enjoyment, celebration, and good company.

When looking at this card on a more esoteric level, it is a very good sign for group work of any kind, be it a medium circle, a coven, or ritual magick group. There is real trust present, and a sense that the members of the group truly know and understand each other. Most importantly, there is a sense of fun, which is a very precious commodity!

If this card is reversed, then it is important not to let partying become over indulgence. When it is negatively aspected, this card may also suggest the first signs of instability and conflict within a group of good friends. Depending on other cards in the reading, it could even indicate a love triangle or illicit affair.

The Three of Swords

In the Three of Swords we return to a solitary figure, his or her suffering evident from the self-destructive pose. As was inevitable, the balance of the Two of Swords has shifted, and somehow this heartbreak has been caused. Because of the nature of the suit of swords, and the qualities of the element of air that it represents, this sorrow is most likely the result of ideas, rather than actions. That is, something may have been said or possibly misheard which has led the mental health of this individual into a downward spiral. The placing of the swords in this image is not intended to purely signify self-harm tendencies, though that is one possible interpretation, but rather the negative nature of the thought processes involved. Two swords are directed at the figure from behind, implying the feeling of being stabbed in the back, perhaps by previously trusted friends. The third sword is in the hands of the figure itself, yet still directed inwards. This implies a certain level of responsibility on the part of the stricken party for the situation that has caused such suffering. The kneeling posture in this case suggests the lack of energy to fight against the negative tide for now, and perhaps a desire to wallow in misfortune. However, it is important to note that the threes are still very early on the sequence, and that we can all survive sorrow and heartbreak, gaining strength and wisdom from the experience.

Divinatory Meaning

In whatever context the Three of Swords may appear, it is likely that someone is experiencing real mental and emotional distress. This could be the result of unfair victimization or bullying in the work place, real or perceived. There is certainly a sense of the Three of Swords feeling as though the world is against them, but not putting up much of a fight. The state of mind indicated by this card suggests someone whose sense of self-worth is currently very low. However, there is great wisdom and understanding to be found by passing through this state. It is hard to feel true compassion, or really appreciate joy, unless you have touched sorrow. That clarity of understanding is the end result of the process spoken about in this card.

In matters of the heart, this card is known to often signify a love triangle, or a break-up of a relationship due to a third party. Though the inevitable period of grief must be lived through, it is better that the truth is now known so that all parties can move on. This card may also signify misplaced jealousy and misinterpreted words or actions.

If the Three of Swords appears in a more spiritual context, it may be a time of facing harsh truths. Perhaps a path or teacher turned out to be unsuitable or even harmful, or a trusted group seems no longer to have good intentions. It may purely be a personal sorrow. There are points in our lives when we may experience what is known as 'the dark night of the soul', and that can certainly fit within the parameters of the Three of Swords. This card may also signify one who is suffering from 'soul loss'—that is when some trauma has caused a part of the individual's soul to break off, leaving them feeling empty, low on energy, and lost. These parts may return in time, or with the help of a shamanic practitioner.

If this card is reversed, it may indicate a high level of insight into a situation, and the ability to see that even though it may hurt, it is better to learn from the truth than to exist undisturbed in ignorance.

The Three of Pentacles

The Three of Pentacles is again a solitary figure, reflecting the pose of the Three of Swords. However, where the Three of Swords was focused inwards, the Three of Pentacles is offering out his achievements to the world. The two pentacles which were the cause of the previous card's dramatic balancing act are now tamed and sitting behind the figure, as he simultaneously admires and displays the results of his efforts. The kneeling pose is not only indicative of the amount of energy that the figure has put into his work, but is also suggestive of supplication to a superior. It almost looks as though the figure is observing his own reflection as he gazes at the pentagram, and in a way he is, for so much of himself has been put into his work. The Three of Pentacles is right to be proud of his creation, for the work is of high quality and any accolade is well earned.

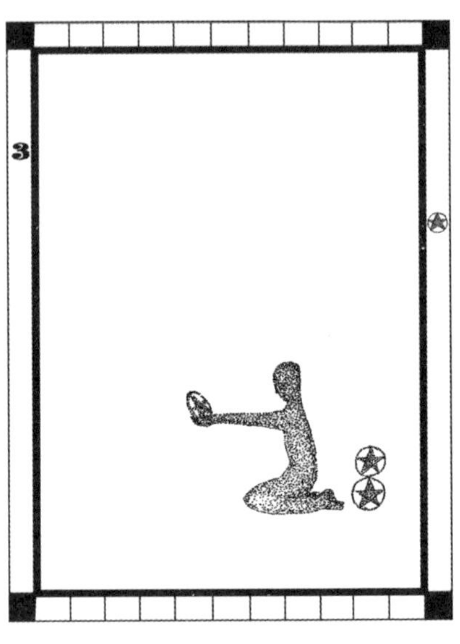

Divinatory Meaning

The appearance of the Three of Pentacles in a reading is a sign that good progress has been made which may attract the interests of a patron or employer. Real talent and enterprise has been shown, and now support is likely to be found which will help it to grow even further. This card shows what can be achieved when passion, intellect, and ability are united with a common purpose. If this card appears at the early stage of someone's career, it shows that not only have they done exceedingly well, but that their efforts have been noticed by others, who will help them to achieve even more in the future. This card may also indicate a good exam result, or a desired university placement.

The Three of Pentacles would be a good sign in a relationship that practical foundations had been laid, and after all the hard work, a period of enjoyment and appreciation of each other's talents will follow.

In magickal or spiritual matters, this card may appear when someone who has worked hard is seen to be ready to move on to the next level. This may be the time when a student can be seen by the teacher to be worthy of more responsibility, and the pathway to deeper knowledge may be uncovered.

If this card should appear negatively aspected, then it may be a case of sloppy workmanship and rushed efforts. The focus has not been present to create something that truly reflects the ability of the querent, and chances of further success and acknowledgement by others will be limited, unless the work is begun again with the proper time and effort spent upon it. It could also mean that someone misguidedly believes they are talented in a particular area when they should perhaps be pursuing other avenues.

The Fours

After the dynamic tension and productivity of the previous small cards, the Fours have finally hit a stable plateau. The energy of the Fours is far more static, and in some cases more introspective than the preceding cards, like a new mother who is finally getting some much-needed rest. Unlike the productive stability of the Threes, the nature of the Fours is far more resistant, and rather reluctant to change. Again, the qualities of the different suits react differently to this new found stability, and it is from these differences we may find the messages of the Fours.

The Four of Wands

In this image we see two figures coming together as one with a common purpose. Each holding two wands in their hands and mirroring the other, they seem to be forming the shape of a house, or at least a rudimentary shelter, with a roof and a doorway. The first stages of established success seen in the Threes are now more secure, and there is not only an increased confidence in ability to achieve, but a trust between partners or a group that comes from experience, knowledge, and

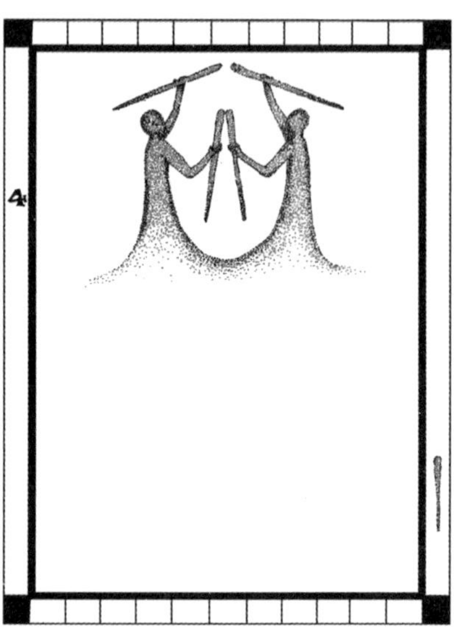

understanding of each other. Now that their skills and qualities are unchallenged, it is time to establish strong foundations for the future, to protect what has already been accomplished, and to provide a platform for further expansion and creativity. Like the two and three before it, the Four of Wands also features a gateway. In this case, however, the gateway seems less like an initiation, as it is sheltered and safe. It is not a gateway to the unknown, then, but rather the beginning of a more secure existence.

Divinatory Meaning

When the Four of Wands appears in a reading, it generally indicates a sense of fulfilment and optimism about the future. This is a card of good health, and that can be applied to both physical health and career issues. The Four of Wands shows that goals have been achieved and now that success can be enjoyed. New businesses have become more firmly established, and new partnerships have blossomed into an enduring team. As this card often signifies the stability of a house or building, perhaps it is time for a business to expand into new offices.

The Four of Wands is a very positive card for those wishing to settle down within a relationship. Traditionally the card is well known for indicating a wedding celebration, but in these modern times of co-habitation it may just as easily be seen as a couple who are moving in to a new home together. It is no stretch of the imagination to also apply this to more established couples finding a new home where they will feel happier, fulfilled, and more secure.

On a spiritual level, this card may indicate someone who feels they have really found their place and role in the world. Both feet are firmly planted on the path, and beliefs and practices are becoming well established. A magickal or spiritual group may have really found its feet and are now able to really work together in love and trust. The establishment of a temple or grove may be indicated.

When reversed, the Four of Wands may warn that stability is not all that it seems. The foundations may not be a strong as was previously thought, and the poor ingredient must be weeded out.

The Four of Cups

Unfortunately, the stability which seemed to suit the Wands so well is not such a good thing when combined with the watery suit of Cups. When water becomes too stable it can become stagnant, and so it is with the Four of Cups. In this card we see an introspective figure examining the contents of one cup, whilst sitting on a much larger chalice. Two smaller cups have either already been examined and dismissed, or remain unnoticed in the background. The sense is that of one who is no longer satisfied with his or her lot in life. Situations which were once fresh and exciting have become predictable and now hold little appeal. Instead of seeing the promise that may be present, the figure has become preoccupied with the details that seem unsatisfactory, and drifts off into endless daydreams. If the time was taken to explore the other cups, particularly the large one on which they are sat, then real possibilities may be uncovered.

Divinatory Meaning

The Four of Cups tends to bring a sense of dissatisfaction and ennui to a reading. In a work situation, the daily grind has become repetitive and no longer challenging. Work no longer seems to engage the imagination, and so there is a tendency to lose concentration. This card may indicate someone who spends more time browsing the internet and doodling than actually working. This is also a concerning card to appear in health issues, as it may indicate an excess of escapist indulgences such as alcohol or drugs. Again, the root cause of such ultimately destructive pursuits is the loss of interest or lack of awareness of what life genuinely has to offer.

Within relationships, the Four of Cups may indicate a similar lack of satisfaction. Lovers may be taken for granted when it seems there is nothing fresh and interesting to explore together, and hearts may wander. There is a tendency to fantasise about the possibilities of an ideal partner instead of seeing the good qualities of the current partner. This card may also appear when someone is unhappy in their single life, yet too full of self-pity to notice the possibilities that are right under their nose!

On a spiritual level, the Four of Cups implies that the spark has gone out of any spiritual path. Somehow dreams have become more appealing than reality, and there is a sense that something is missing. However, if the figure was to only stand up and look around, they would see that they were in fact sitting on the Holy Grail.

If the Four of Cups appears reversed in a reading, then it is a good sign that a stagnant situation will come to an end. Action will be taken to break bad habits, and life becomes full of inspiration and wonder once again.

The Four of Swords

The journey of the Swords suit so far has not been an easy one, and here we can take a well-earned rest. Stability in the mental realm of the Swords manifests itself as a time of repose after the struggles and sorrow of the preceding cards. In the Four of Swords we see a figure lying, almost tomblike, upon one sword, whilst three further swords point outwards, protecting the resting figure from any interference. The outside world is kept at bay for the time being, and the mind is able to find peace and quiet.

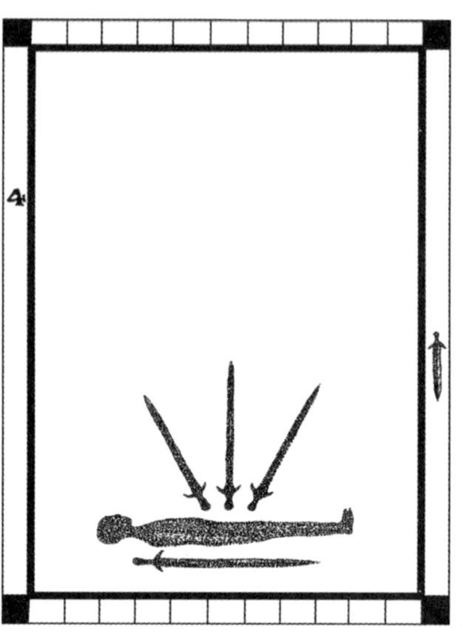

Unlike the daydream escapism of the Four of Cups, this escape is much needed in order to recover and reflect on what is past, and in order to allow any wounds to heal. It is also interesting to note that the three swords pointing outwards seem to form the druidic symbol of Awen, which represents the breath of inspiration. The stillness of thought found in the Four of Swords allows fresh and more positive ideas room to breathe, and may even result in the light of true divine inspiration.

Divinatory Meaning

The essential quality of the Four of Swords within a reading is that of a much-needed retreat from the world after a period of much anxiety and upset. On a basic level, it could indicate the need for a break from work after a period of stress and difficulty. If work has been making unreasonable demands on the querent's time, then this card shows that it is time for personal needs to take priority, otherwise health may be seriously affected. This card may also appear when health has already become an issue, and shows that what is needed to gain strength is a time of rest and relaxation.

If the Four of Swords appears within the context of relationship advice, then it may indicate the need to respect each other's space and boundaries. It may also speak of the need to get away for some quiet time together, away from the demands of others and the strains of daily life.

Spiritually, this is the card of meditation and reflection. After a time of questioning, struggle and torment, inspiration and healing may be found through a time of stillness and contemplation. If the self has been feeling fragmented, the peace of the Four of Swords can lead to its restoration.

If the Four of Swords is reversed in your reading, it is time to re-enter the world after a period of absence, bringing renewed optimism, vitality, and strength. Wisdom gained through meditation and dreams may be applied practically in the everyday world.

The Four of Pentacles

The stable nature of the Fours combined with the naturally-stable element of earth create in the Four of Pentacles a card which is so stable that it seems unwilling to move at all! In this image we can see a figure possessively clinging to one pentacle as it keeps another two firmly under his right foot. A fourth pentacle seems to crown the figure as it rests on his head. Much was gained during the processes of the earlier cards in the sequence, and now it is being fiercely protected. From the pose of this figure,

we can see that little is likely to escape his grasp, but he is also limited as to what he is open to receive. Although there is definitely a sense of pride and achievement present in this image, there is little sense of real enjoyment, and certainly no hint of the wealth being shared. It will also be difficult for the figure to continue to be creative when he is so occupied with protecting his gains. In order for his prosperity to continue, he will have to learn to trust others and share not only his skills, but that which he has gained by them. If he does not do so, he risks a solitary and unrewarding existence, always fearing the loss of his wealth rather than enjoying the comfort and opportunities it could bring to himself and others.

Divinatory meaning

On one hand, the Four of Pentacles can be a very positive card to see in a reading, as it indicates that not only has much been gained, but that it is safe and unlikely to be lost. On the other hand, however, this card carries a warning that if we are unwilling to share what is earned we may become weighed down by it. This card is most likely to pertain to money matters, where the obvious interpretation is that despite material wealth being plentiful, there is a reluctance to part with any amount of it, thus giving the impression of someone who is a bit of a 'scrooge'. This could be due to motivations as simple as greed, or it could be due to fear of earlier times of struggle returning. Unfortunately, this could become a self-fulfilling prophecy, for although the situation is stable, it is also forcibly static, which makes it difficult for new growth to enter. Eventually, what has been clung to so severely may wither for lack of space to grow and flourish.

These tendencies would be particularly concerning within a relationship, where the Four of Pentacles could easily be hinting at possessiveness and jealousy. There may also be a lack of ability to trust which can be very damaging to any friendship or romance, as well as a reluctance to share wealth and possessions.

On a spiritual level, this card could warn of an overly materialistic attitude. It could also hint that although much has been learned, there may be a tendency to hoard power rather than using it to help others.

When reversed, this card may indicate the loss of financial stability that was taken for granted, or else an act of great charity, depending as always on the surrounding and combined cards.

The Fives

In the Fives we see the appearance of an unforeseen difficulty which serves to tip the almost complacent stability of the fours into disarray. No matter how established any situation is, there must always come a time of challenge in order that new life lessons are learnt, and more self-knowledge is gained. It is often life's failures and mistakes that teach us our most valuable lessons, and it is these episodes of life that are dealt with in the Fives. These are the experiences that truly temper us and make us stronger. By testing all that we have come to rely on, the Fives help us to contact the real source of our inner strength—spirit.

The Five of Wands

In the Five of Wands we see a figure struggling to maintain control under an onslaught of rival wands. The overall image is chaotic and unbalanced, as is the energy this card portrays. Although there is not really a strong sense of violence in this onslaught, there is a need for the figure to prove his worth above the others, showing that he stands above the competition. The figure may well have his goal clearly in sight, but his progress is hampered by having to deal with what

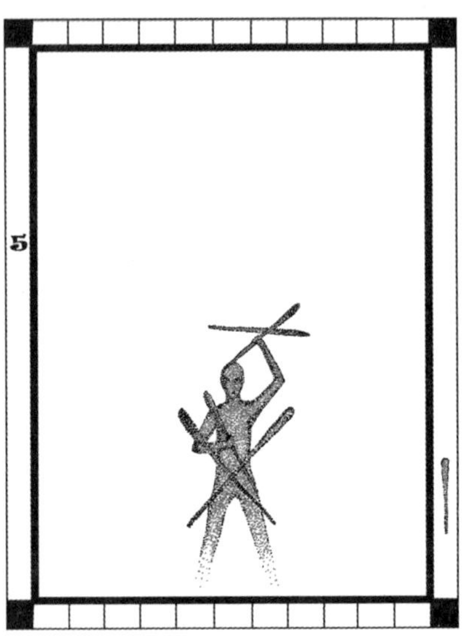

may amount to be a series of very minor conflicts. The repeated pattern of the wands being crossed in front of him may be seen to symbolise this frustration. However, he does not appear to be under threat of being completely overwhelmed. If he can find his inner balance, confidence, and serenity, then not only will he be able to maintain his dignity, but may well emerge the victor. If a warrior is never challenged, how is he to prove his skill and ability? Though the experience of the Five of Wands can feel like an unnecessary distraction at the time, it is an important step towards true respect and recognition.

Divinatory Meaning

When the Five of Wands appears in a reading, then it generally indicates an atmosphere of annoying or sometimes even playful status struggles. On a minor scale, it is likely to indicate competition between associates or even business partners; on a larger scale it may show rivalry between businesses. People may be competing for work or the attention of clients, or it may even speak of a student wishing to prove his ability above his classmates. Although it is unlikely to come to anything too serious, this rivalry may include a tendency to try and put each other down in order to come out on top. This card may well be speaking of someone who finds themselves in a management position over a group of people to whom he needs to work hard to prove himself. It is important to maintain integrity and inner strength during these times of challenge, and not to lash out in desperation.

The Five of Wands could also indicate annoying everyday factors which prevent a couple from enjoying each other's company. Within this more emotional context, it is possible also that there is more than one individual competing for the attention of a romantic interest! Again, it is the strength of truth and spirit that will win this struggle, and not the vain efforts of showy tactics.

Similarly, it may be difficult to find time for spiritual pursuits when we are beset by the distractions of the Five of Wands. At these times it is important to realise that there may be spiritual lessons found in the most unlikely of circumstances. If this card appears to signify status struggles within a spiritual or magickal group, (for these often occur), it is best to rise above it and not indulge in any foolish shenanigans. A truly spiritual person knows that they have no need to prove or justify themselves to their peers.

If the Five of Wands appears to be negatively aspected within a reading, then it is possible that what appear to be obstacles to progress are within the querent's own mind and pose no real threat. Problems are being generated from within and may be overcome with increased self-knowledge and awareness.

The Five of Cups

The diminutive figure of the Five of Cups is so lost in self-pity that he seems reluctant to take up any space on the card at all! What was taken for granted or ignored in the Four of Cups has now been lost, and it is finally and profoundly missed in its absence. However, there is still an unseen hope present, for behind the mourning figure and the two fallen cups stand three upright cups. In those cups may be found the companionship and joy of the Three of Cups, once the feeling of loss and dejection has passed.

As the cups are the suit of water and the emotions, this card carries the weight of real depression at what has been lost. Under such a weight, it can be very difficult to see the good things that may still be left, but it is important to remember that what is lost will in time make room for new growth and happiness.

Divinatory Meaning

This card teaches us that obsession with what has been lost or is absent may lead us to neglect the positive things which still remain. On a physical level this could indicate someone who becomes so hung up on a health problem that they cannot see or implement the simple solutions that are right under their nose. An example of this may be someone who comfort eats because they are depressed about a weight problem. Within a work situation, perhaps someone is dwelling on a project which failed, rather than spending their time on more promising current and future enterprises.

Often the Five of Cups may speak of an individual who is so consumed by the failure of one relationship, that he or she cannot see the bright new possibilities that are so close. So attached to that which has been lost, they are unwilling to entertain the thought of moving on, which can leave them feeling as if they are in a sort of 'no-man's land'. Though one love may have been lost, there is someone who may always have been present, waiting for the right time to come forward. Once reasonable time has been taken to heal the emotional wounds of the past, the time must come to leave them behind and open up to the potential of the future.

There is a real possibility for spiritual growth to be found in the acceptance of loss. Dwelling on failure is a pre-occupation of the ego, and can be overcome with a more expansive outlook. This is an experience that can lead to greater wisdom and understanding of life, and open an individual up to greater wonder and appreciation of the good things that life has to offer.

When reversed, this card may indicate that something or someone which was thought lost may be about to return. Depending on the associated cards, however, it may also indicate that so much time has been spent dwelling on what is missing, that it may be too late for the opportunities offered by the remaining three cups.

The Five of Swords

The image displayed in the Five of Swords is quite clearly not an optimistic one. Here we see a figure apparently in the aftermath of a confrontation in which not only is he not the victor, but his weapon is completely shattered. Because the swords are related to the element of air and thus the mind, it is unlikely, though not impossible, for it to have been a physical fight. It is more likely that the swords here represent a point of view, a principle, or a line of reasoning which has been not only countered, but well

and truly trampled on. The unseen victor in this situation may well be considered a bully for the unnecessary extent to which he has hammered home the defeat of his opposition. Perhaps it would have been wiser for the querent to spend more time in the recuperation shown in the Four of Swords, but he or she has tried to face a challenge which they are not ready for. The posture of the figure shows that little hope remains and that he is no longer even willing to fight. Certainly one of the lessons offered by this card is that fighting is not always the best option when faced with impossible odds. Not every battle can be won, and it may be more prudent to conserve strength for those in which it can really make a difference.

Divinatory Meaning

Through this card we may learn what it means to face insurmountable odds. On a physical level, it may appear in the case of an illness which is proving difficult to beat. It may also point to the loss of a legal dispute or court case in which the opposition plainly has the upper hand. In this situation, this card may advise that it would be better not to pursue the matter at all, and to conserve resources and dignity. It is a card which may appear if someone is being bullied at home, school, or work, and suggests the best solution may be to try not to engage in any conflict with them. As it is a card which deals with mental states, it may indicate someone whose lack of drive and success in life is due to their own negative attitude, creating their own worst enemy in themselves.

The Five of Swords may appear in a relationship reading if someone feels constantly put down or even abused by their partner. It certainly is not an indicator of a healthy and balanced relationship, and it may be wiser to try and leave the situation before it degenerates even further.

If it is spiritual ideals that are challenged in the Five of Swords, then it is a reminder that there is no need to fight those who do not understand or agree. The only person who needs to acknowledge and embrace your beliefs is yourself.

When the Five of Swords is reversed, it may well be that it is the querent who has emerged victorious in this situation, but at what cost? This card warns us not to cause unneeded suffering in the wake of our success, and to not gloat on the defeat of others.

The Five of Pentacles

In the Five of Pentacles we see a forlorn figure sitting humbly in the corner of the card. He sees nothing before him, but is supported from behind by five unseen pentacles. Pentacles are associated with physical well being and wealth, but also with the season of winter. It is this latter association which is most pertinent with this card, for it speaks of a loss which is temporary and seasonal. We all go through such difficult times, when we must struggle with low funds or perhaps an illness. Though the figure is facing

a time of hardship, it is through the lack of physical comfort that they may discover the deep inner strength of their spirit. The support will be there when they need it most, and soon the spring will come again, with new growth and opportunities. Like all of the Fives, this card poses a challenge, but it also speaks of great hope for the future.

Divinatory Meaning

The Five of Pentacles usually signifies a time of physical hardship. This could be due to a sudden drop in finances, for example the loss of a job or even a home. These losses are most likely to be naturally occurring and cyclic, for example, a business folding, or the end of a rental contract on a property. This card may also signify the loss of good health for a while. There is not a sense of any malignant entity being responsible for these hardships, and they are the sort of things that could happen to anyone at any time. The important thing to remember is the opportunity that is offered by the absence of certain luxuries and even necessities. It is these times of difficulty that teach us where our true strengths lie, and who we can depend on when we need them most. As the figure is supported by the five pentacles, so we all may feel the support of others, the guidance of spirit, and discover our most profound strengths.

If a couple can support each other through such difficult times, they will surely emerge the stronger for it as a result. A family may experience lean times, but they will surely pull together and find a way to survive. The Five of Pentacles is surely a cloud with a silver lining, for real depth of trust may not always be discovered unless it is really tested.

There is a very strong spiritual aspect to this card, and although its lessons are normally enforced by the natural ebb and flow of life, it may in some cases suggest voluntary abstinence from certain comforts in order to better access and understand the deeper levels of existence.

When reversed this card may indicate that the lean times are coming to an end, and that wealth and good health are waiting just around the corner. However, if combined cards leave the Five of Pentacles seriously ill-aspected, then it may be not only physical well-being, but also spiritual matters that are at a low ebb, and the querent may struggle to find the support that they so badly need.

The Sixes

The Sixes return again to balance, having integrated the lessons of the preceding cards. When all the Sixes are seen together like this, they almost look like a crown or trophy, and there is certainly the sense that after a time of great challenges, the sixes have come out on top. They have each found a solution to their problems, in accordance to the nature of their suit. They carry with them the wisdom of experience, and a higher level of empathy and generosity due to having survived the trials of the Fives. Rather than returning to the solid stability of the Fours, the Sixes move forward into a harmony built of compassion and understanding. The Sixes are able to acknowledge that the hardships they have experienced were necessary in order to make them complete and are able to look back on them as part of the greater tapestry of life.

The Six of Wands

From the power struggle of the Five of Wands, the Six of Wands emerges victorious. The two wands which were previously deflecting blows are now held in a heroic pose, and the wands which had formerly been antagonistic are now supportive and part of the whole. As is appropriate for fiery wands, this card shows a victory earned through energy and charisma. The wands which support the figure demonstrate that the competition have been rightfully vanquished, and are even happy to acknowledge him as their champion.

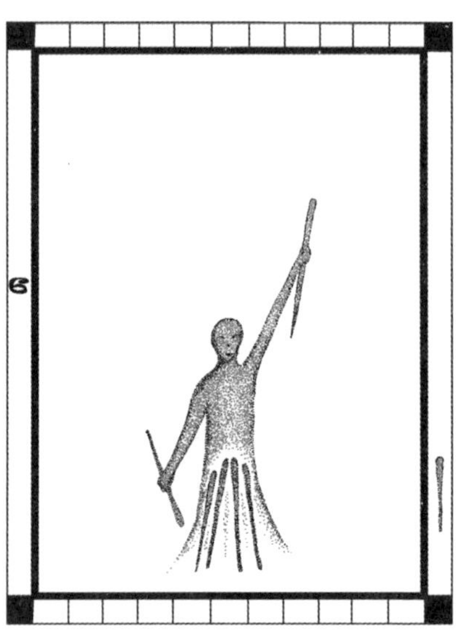

The figure's pose also suggests a strong connection to spiritual guidance, with one arm pointing down to earth and the other to the heavens. It is this ability to integrate and properly channel his creative and dynamic energies that have raised the Six of Wands to a higher status. In some cases, there may even be an amount of fame attached to this success, as the suit of Wands in such a favourable aspect is a powerful and attractive force.

Divinatory Meaning

The Six of Wands is nearly always a welcome sight in any reading, signifying spectacular and well-earned success. If there have been disagreements in the workplace, for example on which the direction a business or project should be taking, the Six of Wands brings an exciting and cohesive solution that will move things forward and upwards. The individual signified by this card is potentially a great leader in any situation. On a grander scale, therefore, this card may signify success in an election. As the Wands are also packed with creative energy, the Six of Wands may signify the leading role in a play or film, or accolades and exposure for an artist or writer.

There is certainly a phallic quality to the Six of Wands that cannot be ignored if reading about relationship issues. Certainly this card may signify prowess in the bedroom, and a new lease of life for any romance which has been experiencing difficulties. For new relationships however, there may be a hint of conquest associated with the Six of Wands, as if a partner has finally been 'won'. This may be more appealing to some than to others!

This card can also signify a breakthrough spiritual development. Lessons that seemed difficult to grasp at first now finally make holistic sense and may be assimilated. Abilities and skills may become more powerful and effective.

When reversed, the Six of Wands may warn against illusionary success or egomania. This card may also appear reversed if the querent feels they are not worthy or able to succeed, held back purely by their own lack of self-confidence. An individual who works hard, but is unlikely to be noticed may see this card reversed in their reading.

The Six of Cups

There is a pleasant feeling present in the Six of Cups, with a scene that is very open to interpretation. A child holds a small cup in one hand while he either gives, receives, or shares a second cup with an adult figure. The adult figure may be a mother, an older sister, or even a kind teacher, with an air of fondness and approachability. In the skirts of the older figure, we see two cups, symbolising the love and feeling of harmony that they have to share. By the feet of the child are a further two cups, showing that this is a time of plenty and abundant affection. Whereas the Five of Cups signifies loss of love and despair, the Six of Cups explores the contents of those cups which had gone unnoticed behind the despairing figure of the previous card. New friendships, fond memories, and renewed emotional security may all be indicated by this card. The time for grieving is past.

Divinatory Meaning

The Six of Cups presents us with an untouchable moment of happiness. Like the other Sixes, there is an innate sense of harmony and balance as the cups are shared with no boundaries or expectations. The implications of this within a work or financial context may be a secure and supportive environment where people are working towards the greater good. If this card was a job, it would be the kind of job you would always be happy to get up for in the morning, and that you would remember fondly once it had passed. Perhaps a career working towards the betterment of humanity and enhancing the quality of life for others could be indicated.

Traditionally, the Six of Cups is known for signifying the return of loved ones who have been missed, and the possibilities of renewing old relationships and friendships. This card has a lot to give, and no qualms about sharing its emotional wealth. The presence of the shadow of loss can no longer be felt in this situation, which is simply full of the joy of discovering someone to share the beauty and joy of life with.

For spiritual seekers, this card may indicate the return of a soul-mate, or someone with whom mutual spiritual discoveries can be made. There is a strong sense of trust and connection present, which is invaluable. This card may even indicate past life memories, and the opportunity to explore and gain wisdom from them.

When reversed, this card may indicate unwelcome intrusions from the past, or even trauma connected to an unhealthy childhood. What should have been a time of peace and contentment was actually disturbing and damaging, and the past is better left behind.

The Six of Swords

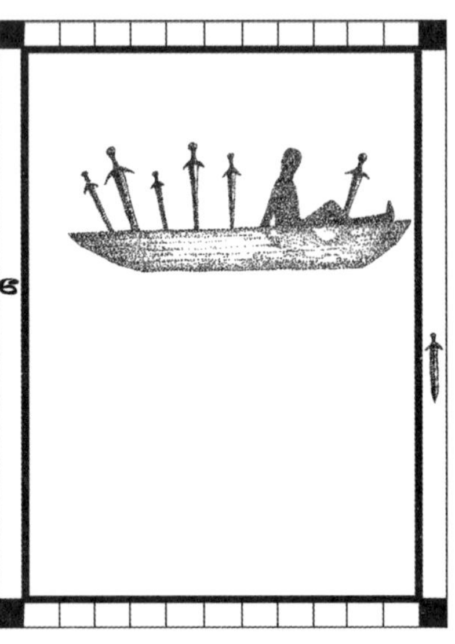

Having survived the potentially humiliating defeat of the Five of Swords, the Six of Swords finds its solution in escape. This is not a rushed or dishonorable exit, but a calculated and logical retreat. The figure on the boat certainly seems relaxed, but watchful, and the waters are still. There are no oars or sails present, as this boat is powered by the will of a focused intellect. The other dimension of possibility here is that the lack of evident means of propulsion shows trust in divine guidance, and that the destination may be in part determined by the fates. Water is symbolic of the unconscious mind and the emotions, so there is sense that the mind is soothed and healed by a new found inner balance and trust in intuition. The calm waters and upright swords show us that whatever the reasons for the journey, it is the act of a sound mind that has come to terms with past difficulties and now wishes to move on. The heartache of the three and the struggles of the five are being left behind. Ahead lies hope for a fresh start and a better future.

Divinatory Meaning

Although the image of the Six of Swords is, of course, symbolic, the obvious interpretation of meaning should not be discounted. This card may often appear in a reading to indicate a journey over water, preceded by a time of stress and difficulties. For example, this card would fit well with a situation where someone decides to take a cruise in order to recover and escape from the stresses of work or personal life. A decision perhaps to move out of an area where there have been troubles may also be indicated, as may a decision to look for a less stressful career. Because of the airy nature of the suit of Swords, these tend to be decisions based on logic and the needs of the mind, rather than practical considerations.

The Six of Swords may indicate successful escape from an unhealthy relationship, with all ties being finally cut. They may not be sure of where they are going, but they know it will be better than where they were. On a less extreme level it could also indicate the need for an individual to have some time away from their partner, or perhaps a couple or family escaping their troubles together and making a new start.

Quite often the Six of Swords does not indicate a physical journey at all, but rather a spiritual journey. Much has happened in the past which may have seemed difficult to understand the reasons for at the time. Through journeying within, or vision questing, answers and support may be found from spirit in order to assimilate and comprehend these experiences. The inner voice can finally be heard now that the waters of the mind, or the querent's thoughts, are still. Once true connection with spirit is achieved, then past troubles can be not only learnt from, but transcended.

When the Six of Swords is reversed, troubles cannot be left behind. They will pursue and resurface until they are faced once and for all. An example of this might be a troublesome ex-boyfriend who becomes a stalker, or when the troubles really lie within the querent and have not been dealt with.

The Six of Pentacles

Mirroring the Six of Cups, the Six of Pentacles also shows an adult figure sharing a moment with a small child. As the suit of Pentacles relates to earthly matters, the difference here is that the card refers very much to sharing of material, rather than emotional, wealth. The woman shown in this card seems to have more than enough for her needs, with five pentacles contained within her robes. Perhaps this shows her recollection of the lean times of the Five of Pentacles? It could be living through that experience which leads her to the generous act of giving a sixth pentacle to the child who has nothing. If we see the child as the recipient, then the woman is offering him a solution to the fallow period shown in the preceding card. However, perhaps it is the child giving his last coin to the adult, showing a gift of exceptional generosity and humble spirit. In contrast to the hoarding nature of the earlier Four of Pentacles, here we can see a fair sharing of resources. Whatever situation it is that this card shows, it symbolizes a return to a balanced state through an act of charity and generosity, whether it be due to calculated reasoning or simple kindheartedness.

Divinatory Meaning

When this card appears in a reading, it may signify the querent being either the generous benefactor, or the receiver of charity. This should be made clear by any combined or surrounding cards, and, as always, the voice of intuition. The Six of Pentacles may as easily signify the act of a larger corporation as that of an individual. An example of this may be an organization which gives a percentage of its profits to charity, or even a charitable organization itself. This card also may appear for those who give for the more cynical reason of significant tax breaks! The Six of Pentacles would be an appropriate card to represent fair trade, showing that both sides of an arrangement are getting a good deal. If the querent is on the receiving end of this sixth pentacle, possible sources are student grants, benefits or inheritance of some kind. Perhaps it may be a simple as a friend or family member offering to help them out of a sticky financial situation.

The Six of Pentacles may also indicate a romantic partnership where one is financially supported by the other. This is often the case if one of the couple is studying or still searching for appropriate work, or if they opt to stay at home to raise the children. Unless indicated by other cards, then it is a fair and balanced situation.

The more spiritual dimension to this card speaks of an act of Karma. Generosity and acts of kindness bring rewards in time to those who tender them.

If the Six of Pentacles appears to be reversed, then there is a reluctance to give. Perhaps government benefits which are rightly owed are not forthcoming, or a wealthy person begrudges giving any small amount to charity. Returning to the image in the card, the woman would be taking the last pentacle from the child, motivated by greed and little thought for the child's welfare.

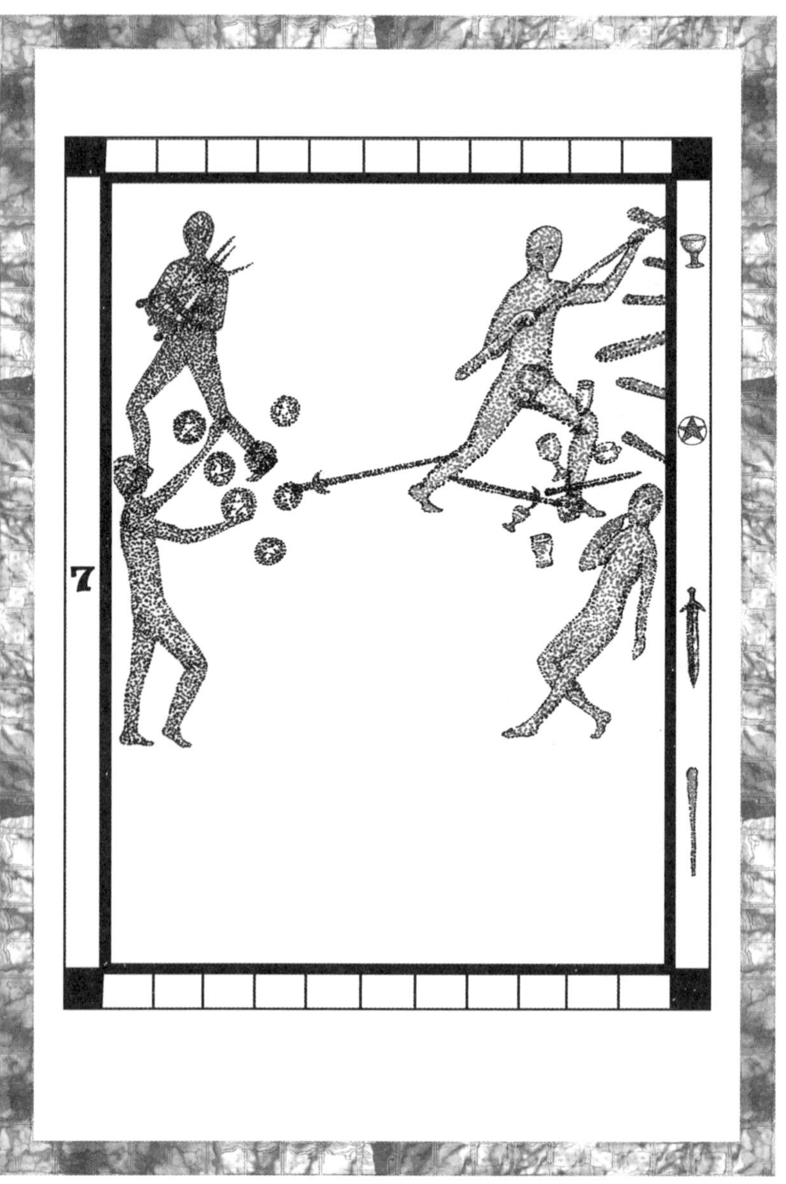

The Sevens

The Sevens can be difficult to interpret as they speak of actions and processes which are happening behind the scenes or under the surface, and are seemingly out of the conscious control of the querent. The challenge of the Sevens is to face up to the mysterious forces which they represent on their own ground, using the innate energy of each suit to integrate and find control over the situation. Seven is well known to be a powerful magical number, even on the most basic level of 'lucky seven'. The Sevens of Tarot manifest that power by teaching us important lessons about the nature of each element, and how to access and use their energies within us.

The Seven of Wands

Each expansion from a position of stability brings its time of struggle as the status quo rearranges itself. Although the Seven of Wands may seem reminiscent of the power struggles and frustration of the Five of Wands, in this case the energies are more focused and hence more of a threat to individual control and leadership. In contrast to the mess of wands all vying for attention in the Five, the Seven of Wands shows us a dynamic figure battling valiantly with his one wand against six wands which seem very much focused on his downfall. Despite the overwhelming odds, the figure seems to be handling the situation well, relishing the challenge. This is a portrayal of a true warrior, who is able to use the fire and focus of his enemies against them, displaying his prowess and worth. The victory of the Six of Wands has drawn attention to him as a leader, and he must continually prove himself in order to not only keep his position, but protect those who are his responsibility. His pose is solid, yet full of action, with no thought of retreat. The pressure is on, and there may be a feeling of being swept away by the momentum of events. Success comes from discovering the true strength and exertion of willpower. There is no room for complacency or intellectual discussion within the suit of Wands! Wands are full of passion and action, and this card holds the kind of fire in which heroes are forged.

Divinatory Meaning

The Seven of Wands shows a direct and organised attack upon the querent's status and position, almost like a siege or mutiny. Far from giving in, the querent defends and retaliates valiantly with all he has. If this card seems to be speaking of a career situation, then it may be that a group of people or an organisation is doing its best to knock the querent, or possibly their company, from their current position. It may even be speaking of an unwelcome takeover bid or a legal battle. Although it may seem against the odds, the querent has the energy and drive behind him to make the situation work in his favour, and to prove his worthiness once more.

If the Seven of Wands should appear in relation to health matters, it could indicate a serious health problem or illness which may be overcome despite professional opinions. The querent has incredible strength of will and the spirit to come through these difficulties to a full recovery.

This card may also indicate objections from family or society towards a relationship, perhaps for race, class or religious reasons. Again, though there will be difficult times, the right side will win through. The querent has truth and conviction on his side, and a spirit which will not be quelled.

Perhaps it is the querent's faith or beliefs which are challenged. In this case, the strength they draw from those very beliefs will be enough to carry them through such difficult times.

However, if this card appears reversed, then it is an indicator of a lack of strength in the convictions of the querent. As soon as their position is threatened, then their status will topple, giving in to the opinions and will of the majority.

The Seven of Cups

In the Seven of Cups we see a figure who appears to be almost bowled over by the choices which are being presented to him. All manner of different cups float before him, and he is rendered unsure to the point of inaction. There is a suggestion in the figure's limp and unbalanced gait which implies he may already be under the influence of certain substances, and could possibly be hallucinating. There is certainly the implication not only of over indulgence, but of the dangers of illusionary promises present in this card. The

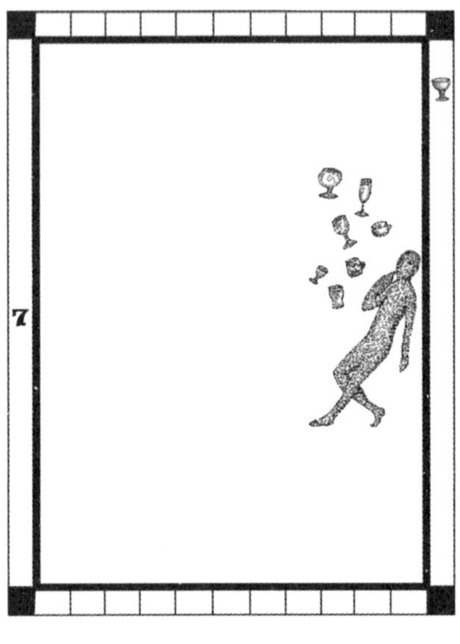

figure looks as though he is literally being pushed off his feet by the hovering cups, almost as if they are bullying him into making a decision. There can be a sense of magical enchantment that accompanies this card, which is enjoyable at the time, but is not a sustainable state. Cups is the suit of emotions and intuition, and if the querent is to find a safe path through this forest of illusions, then he must trust his own intuition to guide him. Choices which look appealing may just not feel right, and the time must be taken to feel the way through the situation, as other senses may not be trusted.

Divinatory Meaning

When the Seven of Cups appears in a reading, care must be taken that daydreams do not take over completely from tangible reality. Although dreams and imagination feed our spirit and creativity, there must always be a balance kept with the laws and needs of physical reality. This card usually implies that the balance is threatened, and the line between fantasy and reality is becoming blurred. Although fantasising about possible futures and opportunities is appealing, it can interfere with work that needs doing in the present. Some dreams may well be attainable, but nothing comes without work and practical application. In the workplace, this card warns of the perils of flights of fantasy, advising the querent to keep his or her feet on the ground. Perhaps there are rumours or possibilities being hinted at, but it is important not to get carried away by a tide of excitement until they manifest as something tangible. This could be a worrying card to receive in relation to health matters, as it often implies escape into drugs or alcohol. As illusions become more appealing than reality, the querent slowly loses touch with their physical body and its needs.

In matters of the heart, the querent may be tempted by exotic promises or attractive flirtations. It is important to look beyond the surface to the emotional reality, as true substance may be lacking. The querent must take the time to discover which offers are truly valid, lest they abandon real affection for the lures of glamorous delusion.

When spiritual perception starts to really open up within an individual, it can start to feel very much like the Seven of Cups. The imagination is a powerful perceptive tool, but it can sometimes be unruly. It is through disciplined intuition and enlightened questioning that the true path may be found.

When the Seven of Cups appears reversed in a reading, then the querent may feel that no options are open to them. Perhaps they have already pursued an illusionary grail and found it to be empty, resulting in distrust and despair. It may also imply a loss of hope due to alcoholism or drug addiction, to the extreme of dependency that occurs when the highs can no longer be reached.

The Seven of Swords

A figure tip-toes stealthily off the card with four swords in his arms, glancing over his shoulder at the remaining three which lie on the floor. Perhaps he has accidentally dropped them as he makes his escape, or perhaps he is wondering if he can manage to take the extra swords as well. One thing which is almost certain with the Seven of Swords is that these swords have probably not been gained by the most honest and direct means! Although it may be the querent who is acting dishonestly, this card usually indicates unseen forces at work which may threaten to undermine the querent's situation. Although traditionally this card is known to warn of potential theft, be it of property or reputation, it may also signify anything from sophisticated espionage to damaging gossip. The more positive aspect of this card speaks of careful strategy and the need to remain undiscovered. As with all the Sevens, the essence of the card must be embraced in order to combat it. This means that in order to uncover the mystery and expose the thief, it is necessary to employ an even more cunning and sly approach. With this in mind, we can see that the three swords on the floor may represent a potential trail to follow—but has it been deliberately placed in order to mislead? The Seven of Swords advises us to question everything.

Divinatory Meaning

If the Seven of Swords sneaks its way into your reading, then it might be a good time to grow eyes in the back of your head. All is not what it seems, and there is intense activity beneath the surface of apparent events. Of course, if it is combined with incredibly positive cards it could be something as innocent as friends organizing a surprise birthday party. It is also possible to harness the qualities of this card for honorable purposes, if there is work that needs to be done which must remain hidden, or that requires intense strategic planning. If the feeling is that less noble actions are indicated, then perhaps someone within the querent's company is embezzling funds, or plotting to do so. Another possibility is that someone is spreading vicious gossip, intending to damage the querent's good standing. Being an air card, and thus related to the actions of the intellect, perhaps it is ideas which are being stolen. Or the card may simply warn of a potential burglary or theft. In any event, the querent would be well advised to be on their guard and pay attention to any little details which may give away the truth of the situation.

The Seven of Swords has also been known to speak of potential dishonesty within relationships. On an obvious level it may indicate adultery, or at least that not all in the relationship is what it seems. Conversely, it may also be warning that the querent's partner suspects them of something, and rather than confronting them, is sneaking about reading diaries and spying on them. It is also not out of the question that this card may be warning of a stalker, or possibly even the rather modern threat of identity theft.

There are also many possible interpretations for this card within a more spiritual context. Be careful of people who seem pleasant but are draining to be around—they may be taking your energy. Ancient secrets may be discovered, but most likely through unconventional and original methods. Things may seem unclear and mysterious, and it is important to look below the surface of the everyday to uncover the truth.

When the Seven of Swords is reversed in a reading, it may well bring recent underhanded activities into the light of day. This is wonderful news if the querent is innocent, but if the querent is the guilty party, then they are likely to be caught red-handed!

The Seven of Pentacles

At first glance this card may seem similar to the Seven of Cups, as the seven pentacles hang invitingly before the figure. However, we can see that in this case, not only are the pentacles tangible and real, but the stance of the figure is more grounded and alert. The Seven of Pentacles is not intended to portray a baffling array of choices, but rather the fruits of diligent labor, which will soon be ready for harvest. The figure inspects his potential crop, notes how they are developing, and chooses which might be 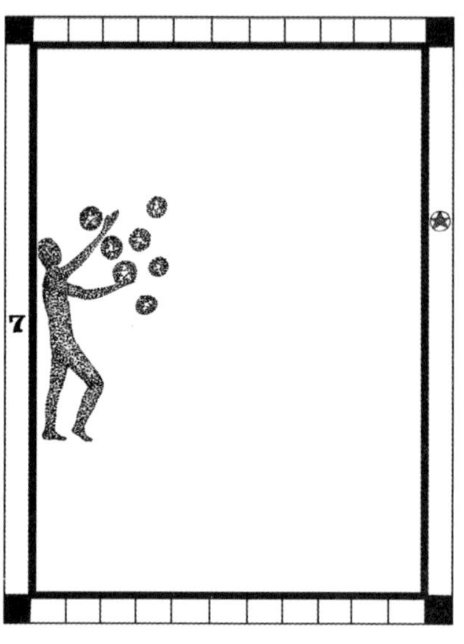 ready to be picked. The unseen process of this card is the process of all growing things, as is fitting for the earthy suit of Pentacles. If we stand and watch a plant, we may not notice its growth, but if we note its progress over a period of time, then its rate of growth may be truly impressive. The key principles here are hard work, care and patience, which will bring rich rewards if adhered to. It is as though the child of the Six of Pentacles has taken his one pentacle, planted it, and tended it over many years. There may be times when he has been tempted to pluck the fruit before it is ready, but then all would be lost. The Seven of Pentacles teaches us that if we can maintain our efforts and patience just a little longer, then well-earned success is due.

Divinatory Meaning

The Seven of Pentacles may appear in a reading when patience and effort are about to show their worth. It may signify a financial investment such as shares or bonds which are soon to pay out, or could even be as literal as an actual harvest. Whatever the querent has put into a project, pastime, or job is about to ripen and share its fruit. Provided that due care and attention has been taken, and nothing has been rushed, then the rewards will be well worth all the effort that has been put in.

Perhaps the Seven of Pentacles may show a relationship which has improved with age, or perhaps shows a long engagement which is finally ready to make the leap into marriage. Long term happiness within a relationship means that it must be continually worked on, and not taken for granted. Many joyous anniversaries may be the fruit indicated by this card.

Spiritually, this card shows us that if we develop our skills with patience, keeping our feet on the ground and staying rooted within nature, exceptional results will manifest in time. Always rushing to the next lesson or initiation may lead to holes in our understanding and sloppiness of practice.

If the Seven of Pentacles appears reversed within a reading, then there is a danger of the crop being ruined by over-eagerness or greed. Trying to grab at fruit before it is ripe leaves a bitter taste and wasted effort.

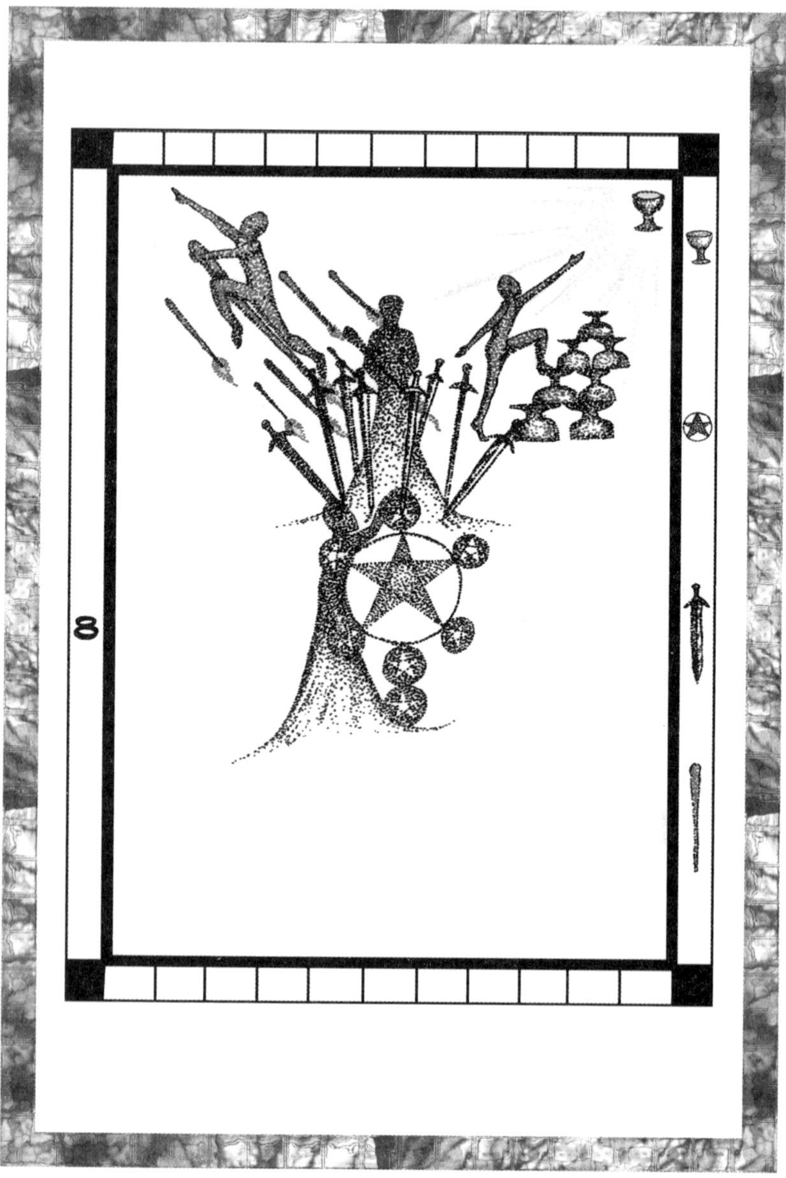

The Eights

The Eights all represent major transitions of life, and growth through movement. They now have passed through many trials and successes, and act according not only to the nature of their suit, but also with the wisdom of their experiences to guide them. The transitions signified by the Eights are not enforced by circumstance or random twists of fate, but rather are the result of exertion of individual will. In some cases, as it is with life, the movement meets with little resistance. In others, the decision to change can be hard and even painful. What is true of all these cards, though, is that they bring the opportunity for deep inner transformation and empowerment.

The Eight of Wands

This fiery card exudes movement and transformation from every cell of its being. A figure rides a great wand like a jet-powered broomstick, while seven further wands join them on their meteoric rise up into the heavens. The Eight of Wands is packed full of almost explosive energy, which may not be sustainable for a long period, but may achieve much in a short time. Like the figure riding the wand in the image, it is an energy we can embrace and direct to reach our 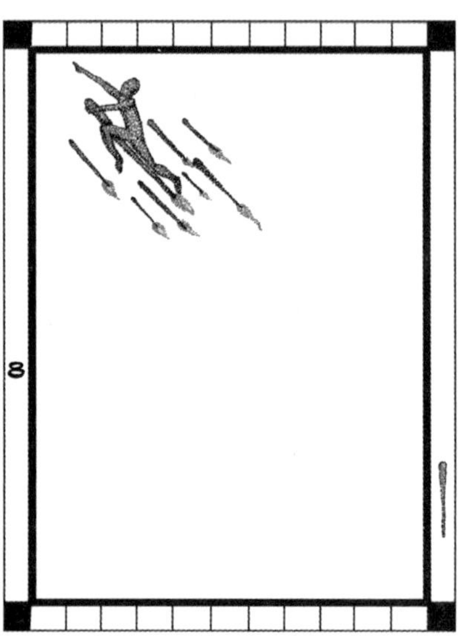 goals. As he rides the energy of the eight wands, the figure points the way ahead, showing that his goal is in sight and that he is in control. Fire is the element of transformation, so it is fitting that out of all the Eights, this card seems to contain the least obstacles or complications in its journey. Any threat or competition has been left far behind, and with the proper focus, the Eight of Wands has the power to bring about incredibly rapid progress.

Divinatory Meaning

When the Eight of Wands appears in a reading, then it's time to hold on tight and prepare for a ride! This card speaks of a period when, possibly after a time of frustration and complications, everything seems to happen at once. The fog dissipates, and the path ahead is clear and uncluttered. This is a time of hectic communications, with exciting events unfolding at a dramatic pace, and the phone constantly ringing. A literal interpretation of the image may suggest air travel, possibly a spontaneous trip with life-changing possibilities. This card has been known to signify acting on a decision to relocate to a new country. It can also show rapid ascension of the career ladder or a change to an exciting new job, possibly involving travel. Whatever possibilities are offered, they are likely to be fresh and inspiring. Old habits and patterns of being are being broken and replaced by dramatic new adventures.

When the Eight of Wands signifies a relationship, it will be the sort of passionate involvement where a couple may be engaged within weeks of meeting each other. Exciting though this may be, it might be advisable to try and slow things down a little, for such a high level of energy cannot be maintained for long. It could even indicate a romantic elopement! If there is a genuine emotional connection present, then the Eight of Wands shows a relationship where boredom is unlikely to be an issue.

On a spiritual level, the Eight of Wands heralds a time of great inspirations, and rapid growth and progress. It is like a door has been unlocked, and for a time the world of spirit and magick seems clear, and great stores of inner power are accessible. Again, it is a transformational experience, but not a sustainable state of being. Like all the eights, it is a phase of transition.

When reversed, however, the Eight of Wands is plummeting down to the ground at speed. Expect complications, delays and possibly even accidents.

The Eight of Cups

Seven inverted cups form a stairway as a figure ascends, reaching for the eighth grail-like cup. Whilst one arm reaches towards his goal, the other stretches behind, as an indicator of the strong attachments which may try to hold him back. The Eight of Cups is a card of reaching for your dreams, but there is a cost, as is implied by the inverted cups. The staircase is formed of the dreams, hopes, and memories of the past. Without them, the figure would not be in the position he is now, but they must be emptied and left behind in order for him to be truly free to reach his goal. However, perhaps these cups were already empty, and by finally accepting that their time has past, he is able to pursue an opportunity for true happiness.

Divinatory Meaning

Although the Eight of Cups carries a message of change for the better, its watery nature means there is an emotional struggle involved. This card may appear when, after many years of trusted service, the time has finally come to leave a firm or company. New opportunities are being offered which will take the querent into a life which up to now they had only dreamed about. However, there are always places and people left behind which must now be consigned to memory, despite accusations of betrayal and disloyalty. This is a card of bittersweet progress and deep emotions.

Traditionally, this card is known to often signify divorce and separation for relationships. Although it may once have been a happy partnership, the waters of the heart have now grown stagnant, and it is time to move on. Although it may seem that one is left behind to suffer while the other escapes to a bright new life, the separation is the healthiest option for all involved. Perhaps the querent has met a new love, or perhaps they wish to simply be alone and independent. Either way, they will find the strength to move on, even though it may cause pain and anger in others. Turning back would only mean artificially sustaining an existence which has already expired.

Another possible interpretation for the Eight of Cups is that the querent has become disillusioned with indoctrinated beliefs or their religion, and wish to seek new, more personal, ways of exploring and expressing their spirituality. Like the Grail quest, it is a journey full of great challenges and deep transformation.

When this card is reversed, the querent has found it too difficult to find the strength needed to escape their present situation. New dreams are sacrificed in order to stay on familiar ground, even if it is becoming increasingly barren and hostile.

The Eight of Swords

In perhaps the most challenging of the Eights, a figure is surrounded by eight swords which seem to pin her to the spot. Her hands are behind her back as though she is bound, so although (like all the Eights) this card is about movement, her movement seems almost entirely constricted. Of course she could just step forward, but what damage may she suffer from the blades of the swords? Yet somehow, she must, for what kind of existence is on hand if she does not? Typical of the suit of Swords, this card dwells in the realm of thoughts and fears, and shows the power they hold over us. Although the figure may be trapped within a very real situation, the barriers holding her back from transcending it are conjurations of an oppressed mind. To defeat that power may be painful and fraught with difficulties, but the potential of freedom makes it worthwhile. The surrounding swords also prevent new life entering as well as leaving. There is no help on offer here—the strength and guidance must be found from within to pass through this phase of hesitancy and doubt. True courage is after all forged not of fearlessness, but of facing up to those fears which are all too real.

Divinatory Meaning

The Eight of Swords shows us that the querent is currently existing in a cage of fears and negative thinking. There is a strong suggestion with this card that the supposed opinions, thoughts, and feelings of others have become an overpowering force which is blocking the querent from achieving his or her goals. An example of this in the workplace would be someone who was full of ideas, but was afraid to share them in case they were laughed at or dismissed out of hand. Perhaps there are indeed people who would disapprove, but the risk must be taken in order for progress to be made. Sometimes it may be something as simple yet as powerful as fear of failure which is holding them back from making a move.

This could also apply within matters of the heart, when fear of rejection can cause any of us to neglect to act at all. The pain of possible rejection must be faced up to in order to be open to the potential joys of love and life. Equally, it is possible that this card could show someone who is trapped in an abusive relationship and fears the consequences of leaving. Though it will be incredibly difficult, that move must be made, or the suffering will continue indefinitely.

The Eight of Swords may indicate that spiritual growth has become hampered by fear of the unknown. Perhaps a frightening spiritual insight or encounter has left the querent doubtful as to how to continue. Once spirit has been perceived, it is difficult to deny it, and yet sometimes visions or perceptions can be truly terrifying. It is a phase that must be moved through in order to reach deeper understanding of the true nature of these experiences.

When reversed, there is no real obstacle to progress. The querent has been hiding behind their own swords and is now free to dismantle their cage.

The Eight of Pentacles

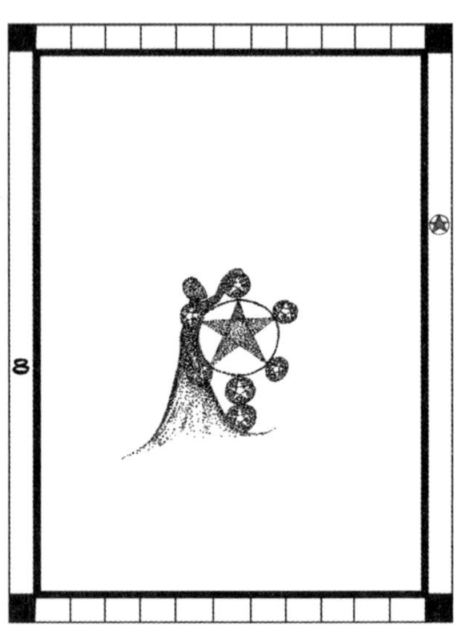

Here we can see a figure putting the final touches into what could be a sculpture or perhaps a piece of machinery. This could well be their masterpiece, combining all the skills and qualities learnt on their journey so far. The Eight of Pentacles represents an opportunity to perfect a skill and share it with the world. Often referred to as the card of the apprentice, this card teaches that attention to detail and commitment to a chosen path can lead to acknowledgement and reward. There may have been many setbacks and moments of disillusionment on the way, but now the end is in sight. The patience demonstrated in the preceding Seven of Pentacles has paid off, and new horizons will soon open up. The apprentice becomes the master, the student becomes the graduate, and the cycle continues on a higher level.

Divinatory Meaning

The Eight of Pentacles appearing in a reading is a sign that it is almost time, in either a literal or symbolic sense, to graduate. The symbolism of the apprentice may be directly applied to the workplace, where after a long period of study, work and perfection of skills, the querent is finally ready to take a place of more authority and well-earned respect. The transition from student to master is indicated by this card, the querent himself being the work in progress which is nearing completion. Perhaps a course or temporary placement will lead to a permanent position within a company and the beginning of a promising career.

Within a more romantic context, this card may show a blossoming relationship moving on to a new stage. The querent has worked patiently upon their skills in romance, and has grown in confidence and ability as a result. Perhaps they have been waiting until finances were more secure, and they will soon propose!

On a spiritual level, this card may indicate that the querent has worked long and hard to master certain disciplines and principles, despite their complexity, and will soon be ready to apply them practically, even possibly teaching others. Tarot and the Qaballah are disciplines which may take such dedication to truly master.

When reversed, the querent fails to graduate. Attention to detail has been lacking and there is not the stamina present to see the project through to the end. All effort to this point has been wasted, and the work must be begun again.

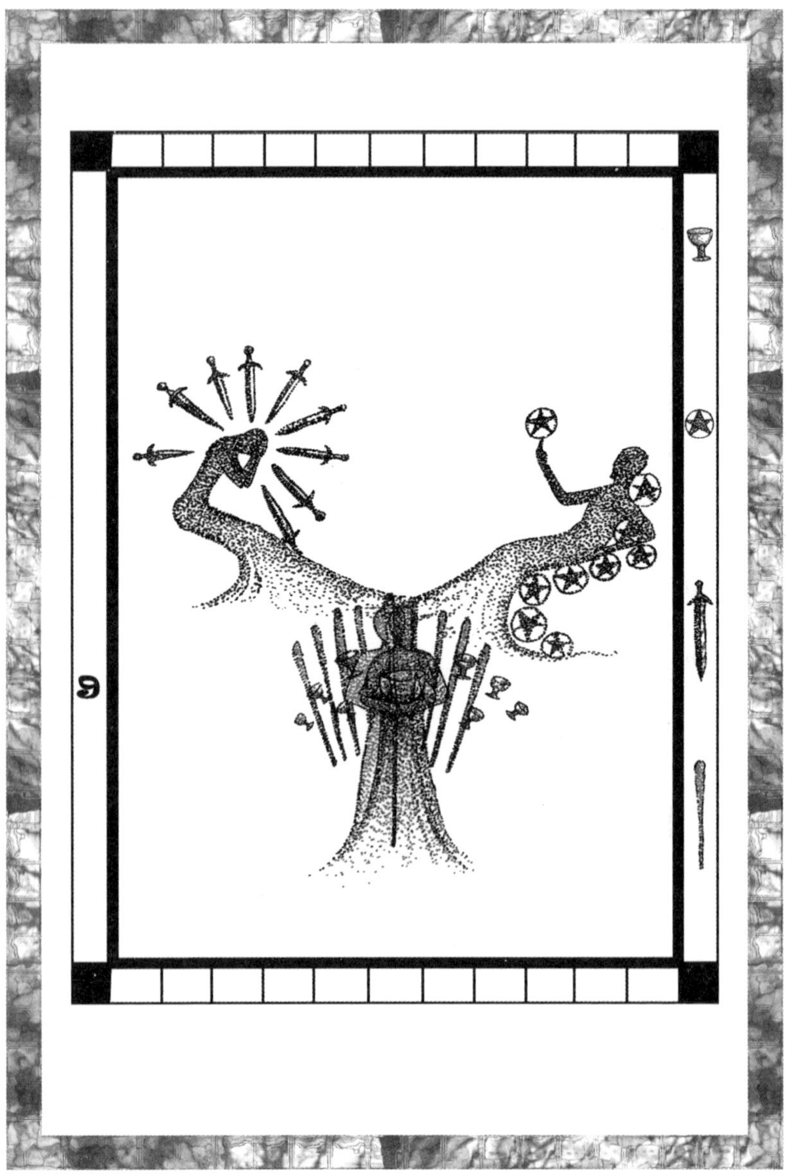

The Nines

Now we are nearly at the end of the journey through the Minor Arcana, and the nature of the Nines reflects that. The end is in sight, be it good or bad, so the Nines all express a sense of fulfilment, or more accurately, self-fulfilling prophecy. It is almost as though they can sense the approach of the Tens and their journey's end, and are preparing themselves for what is to come. Their preparations and expectations actually help to form what will be the conclusion of each suit. There is a sense of approaching completeness, but it is a completeness in which the individual stands alone rather than as part of a team, partnership or unit. For some this will continue to an independent existence, for others it will lead to them being able to welcome others into a secure situation, depending on the lessons that have been learnt through the preceding card of the suit.

The Nine of Wands

In this card we see a figure holding a large wand in a protective stance in front of eight smaller wands. He has come through many battles and has been successful in all of them, and now the situation seems calm and under control. However, he is still standing guard over his achievements, as though he expects further conflicts in the future. His experiences have taught him that when things seem to be stable and going well that there may be unexpected attacks or uprisings around the corner. If we look at his journey so far, this happens from the Four to the Five, and again from the Six to the Seven. Now he has enjoyed the rapid progress of the Eight of Wands, he expects life to follow the same pattern and has prepared for further disruption. He also seems to feel as though whatever may occur, he can tackle on his own, as the eight wands stand behind him, not before him. This is the beginning of taking on great responsibility, and will continue to develop into the next card in the sequence. However it is not clear as to whether the anticipated threat is genuine, or whether he is being over cautious, reluctant to leave his warrior-like role behind.

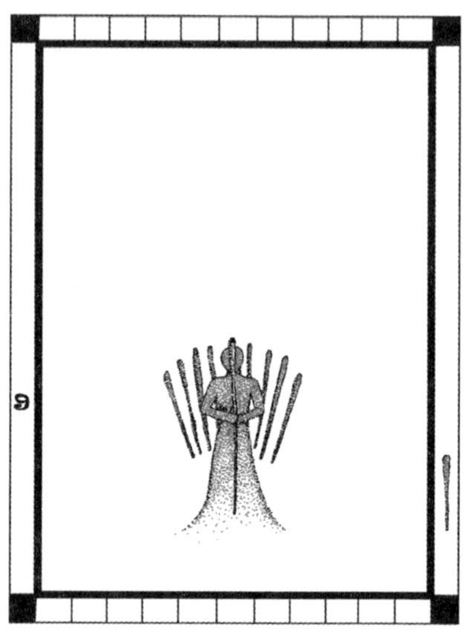

Divinatory Meaning

The Nine of Wands signals a time where the querent may be feeling wary and protective over what is valuable to them, be it money, status, family, or health. Perhaps they have had to fight so hard to get to where they are that they don't know how to stop fighting and settle down. Certainly in career matters, there may have been struggles in the past, and they have emerged victorious. Now that so much has been achieved, there is even more to lose, so the querent has become fiercely protective. It may well be that some threat is about to emerge, such as a young upstart hungry for success that might try to take his job. However, there are no substantial signs of his approach as yet, just a feeling that danger may be approaching.

It may be that this card could arise in relation to more domestic issues. Although it can be nice to feel protected within a relationship, there can be a danger with the Nine of Wands of being smothering or even paranoid and jealous. Another possible perspective is that the querent is so private in his personal life that he or she may find it difficult to let anyone in at all, thus emotionally isolating themselves.

The Nine of Wands may also advise us to work on our spiritual or magickal protection, or be an indicator that there is already strong protection present. However, the flip side of that advice is that too much protection all the time can be not only draining, but also make it difficult for perceptions to be open and sensitive.

The Nine of Wands reversed is likely to manifest the most negative aspect of this card, which is paranoia and isolation. Having shut out the whole world, the querent is left alone. Depending, as always, on other cards, the reversed Nine of Wands may also indicate that attack is imminent and sufficient protection is not yet present.

The Nine of Cups

A central figure holds a huge chalice, surrounded on both sides by eight further cups. At the moment the figure stands alone yet complete, but there is the impression that not only is the large cup being offered, but that the eight cups are waiting for good company to come and drink from them. Again, this is projecting and offering a glimpse of what is to come in the future. After the various emotional challenges and breakthroughs of the suit of Cups so far, the Nine of Cups has finally reached a

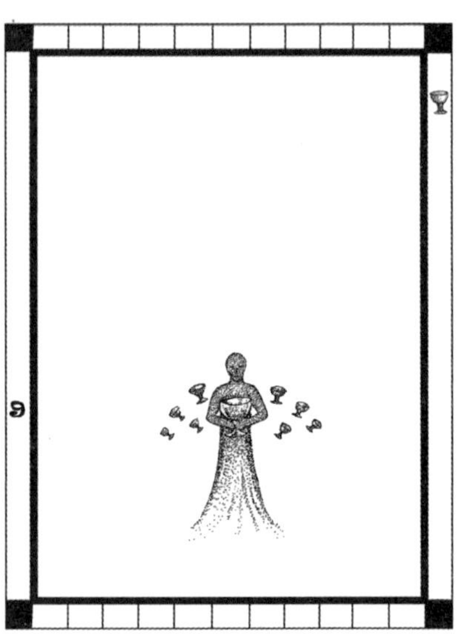

state of emotional wholeness which is not dependant on the opinions or reactions of others. The Grail which was being sought in the Eight of Cups is now held in the figure's hands, and is being offered to all who would drink. Peace and contentment have been achieved, and all those upright cups offer a myriad of possibilities for the future. This position of inner happiness offers a fertile ground in which dreams and wishes really can come true.

Divinatory Meaning
So, what is held in those inviting cups? If it is advice on career or financial matters which is being sought, then this card implies a line of work which brings happiness and creative fulfilment, as well as satisfying any material need there might be. As a Cups card, it primarily speaks of emotional contentment, but if the question is concerning money, then a positive outcome is certainly implied. In fact, the Nine of Cups promises us nothing less than our heart's desire! This also applies in health matters, where the figure is presenting us with the healing Grail. Whatever has been absent will be replenished, and the querent will be whole once more.

This may particularly apply to matters of the heart, where this card shows someone who has finally reached a state where they can be happy with themselves, and so are ready for a relationship which can really last, being based truly on love rather than dependence. The traumatic separation of the Eight of Cups has proven worthwhile, and the querent has found the happiness, security, and freedom they desired.

On a spiritual level, this card has strong associations with the Holy Grail, and the ninefold sisterhood who are its guardians. Many trials and initiations have been passed and now the querent is ready to share their wisdom with the world. Healing may well be indicated, either that the querent will receive the healing they need to become spiritually whole, or that they will be able to heal others.

When reversed, there may still be obstacles in the way of happiness. Promises that inspire dreams may fall through, and social plans become frustrated.

The Nine of Swords

The Nine of Swords presents us with a very different image of fulfillment. Despite brief periods of respite, the journey of the suit of swords has been plagued by fears and disappointments. A figure sits, holding her head in despair and exhaustion as nine swords point inwards towards her head. Here we see someone whose own thoughts have completely turned against them, resulting in paranoia, nightmares and an inability to look up and see the world clearly. In this case, the glimpse of the future has offered only devastation, and the figure is rendered quite incapable of imagining a brighter future. Just as positive visualization and thought can bring about positive events, so such negative thinking can bring about the very occurrences that are feared. The idea of strength in independence that runs through the rest of the Nines is here replaced by loneliness and self-isolation as the suit of Swords demonstrates just how powerful thoughts can be.

Divinatory Meaning

The most comforting thing that can be said about the Nine of Swords in a reading is that the problems really are all in your head! Wherever this card comes in a reading, it generally indicates sleepless nights, constant anxiety, and an inability to think straight. Even if there is real-life cause for concern, it has become blown out of all proportion until it almost becomes an unstoppable demon. If it appears in a question regarding career, then it may indicate that the querent is suffering from stress, finding it difficult not to worry about work, even when they are supposed to be relaxing. A way must be found to leave work behind at the end of the day, otherwise serious mental health problems could emerge. If this card appears to relate to physical health, then it implies a touch of hypochondria, or at least existing symptoms being blown out of all proportion.

When a couple is forced to be apart, then the Nine of Swords will often indicate unfounded fears of awful things happening to the partner while they are away, or worries that they will not be loyal. It is important to remember with this card that it really is the mind generating its own problems, and that there is likely to be no real basis for such exaggerated concerns unless indicated by other cards. However this card can also signify mental cruelty within a relationship, adding another layer of pain onto the situation already seen in the preceding Eight of Swords. It can literally be a 'nightmare' situation.

Similarly, in spiritual matters this card points towards fears of magickal attack which are actually dangerously self-destructive delusions. The querent should spend time grounding and in meditation in order to avoid creating their own negative reality around themselves.

If the Nine of Swords is reversed, then it implies that the querent is waking up to the truth of a situation. They may have been denying the existence of problems for some time, and now reality has come back to haunt them.

The Nine of Pentacles

Reclining luxuriously on eight pentacles, a figure nonchalantly balances one pentacle on the end of her index finger. She appears relaxed and comfortable, with everything she could need. As it is an earthy card, the Nine of Pentacles tends to speak of material and health matters. The time of hard work has passed and it's finally time to enjoy the rewards! All the necessities of life are catered for, and although there is an appreciation of the simple things, there is also more than a little luxury available. The

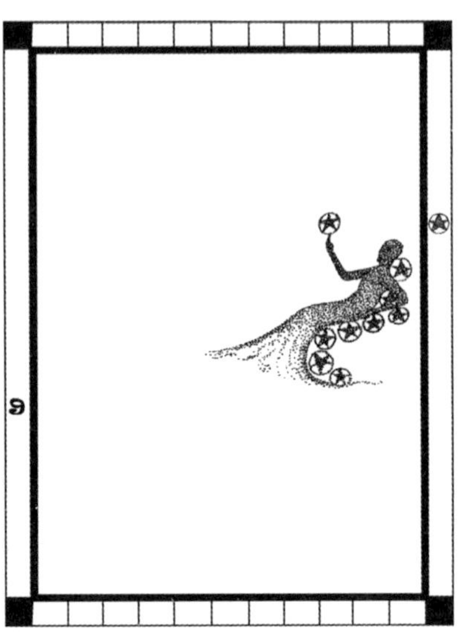

figure is completely supported by the pentacles, showing that the position is comfortable and secure. The extra pentacle being balanced on her finger symbolizes that there is also a little extra to either play with or share with others, should she welcome them into her life. Again, there is a sense of independence with the Nine of Pentacles. If she decides to take a partner or start a family, then it will most definitely be on her terms.

Divinatory Meaning

Obviously this is a very positive card, particularly in physical and financial matters. This card may signal an early retirement or an inheritance which means there is no longer a need to work. At the very least, there should be time for a good holiday without any worries about the cost. The Nine of Pentacles indicates a wonderful quality of life, with a comfortable home. It may speak in a reading of a mortgage being paid off, or an exceptional improvement in health.

For readings regarding relationships, this card could well show someone who is perfectly happy being single. There is a strong aspect of self-sufficiency within this card. If it is someone either within or seeking a relationship, then they are able to provide a stable and happy home as the foundation for their future, possibly even supporting the other partner.

On a more spiritual level, there is a wonderful sense of completeness found from spending time in nature or working with the earth. Perhaps a sense of 'coming home' has been found by exploring nature-based religions.

If this card should appear negatively aspected within a reading, then money may slip easily through the querent's fingers. If the combined cards also suggest it, then there is a possibility that they have gained wealth, but not by honest means. Another possibility is that material gain and comfort does not bring happiness, and there is a sense of loneliness, dissatisfaction, and alienation.

The Tens

At last we come to the end of the journey of the Minor Arcana, and as with all endings, the Tens bring the potential for renewal and the beginning of a new cycle. Just like the daily life which they reflect, it has been quite a roller coaster ride, full of ups and downs and unexpected twists. Looking at the cards combined together, it appears that each of them has finally found its place. The Tens express completion and the conclusion of a chain of events, line of thought or phase of life, all of which are cycles within cycles. For those who believe in the eternal spirit, even one whole life is a smaller part of a greater tale. For some of the suits, their story has a seemingly happy ending. Others have a darker conclusion, but it is important to remember that it is often the troubled times of life that have the most valuable lessons to teach us. All of them have the potential for a bright future ahead of them.

The Ten of Wands

Squashed into the bottom right hand corner of the card, we see a struggling figure bent double as they attempt to carry ten wands. Her arm is stretched towards the ground, either looking for support or possibly even reaching for more weight to add to her burden. The reason for this becomes clear when we look at the preceding cards of the wands suit. Initially, there was the tension and then the thrill of working creatively with others. This produced a wonderful period of stability and enjoyment which became disrupted by trivial squabbles and the struggle to come out on top. Passing through that into leadership and success, the hero of the Wands soon finds themselves the subject of another, more focused attack, in which they have to hold fast and stand for what they believe in. After another brief period of rapid progress, they find themselves once more protecting against anticipated threats in the Nine of Wands. Now, in the Ten of Wands, we can see that they have taken on all the responsibility themselves. This may be because they have learnt not to trust anyone else, or simply because they have proved themselves to be the strongest and most capable through all the trials they have endured and battles they have won. Much has been accomplished, but in the Ten of Wands we finally discover the limits of this fiery suit's capacity.

Divinatory Meaning

The appearance of the Ten of Wands in a reading suggests that the querent has taken on enormous amounts of responsibility and may be having to make sacrifices in order to maintain the necessary level of strength and commitment to the task. This can often be seen in the workplace when someone takes on too much work, and then is surprised to discover that there is actually a limit to their capabilities, no matter how great. The most positive example of this is someone who truly is the only person who can complete a much-needed task and is willing to sacrifice their own well-being in order to help others. A less noble possibility is someone who is highly competitive and insecure to the point where they feel the need to greedily take work from others to make themselves look better. If it is the querent who has taken on all this work, they would be well advised to find a way of delegating or of lessening their load, otherwise they risk stress and exhaustion.

If the Ten of Wands was applied to a relationship, then the implication would be that one member of the partnership took on all the responsibilities and did all the work, leaving the other at leisure. It may be their own choice to do this, perhaps to help someone who is not capable for some reason to do things for themselves. Whatever the reasons may be, the result is an imbalance within the relationship, with one person sacrificing their freedom for the good of the other. The combined cards will help to indicate whether this is a healthy and sustainable situation or not, but certainly the hardworking party should find some way to take a break when they can.

Spiritual and magickal work brings its own responsibilities, and sometimes it can feel as though the weight of the world is on your shoulders. Particularly for those doing healing work within the community, this card is a sign that although the work is important, you must look after yourself as well or you may soon no longer be able to help others. We all have limits, and discovering them is an important step on the paths to truly knowing ourselves.

When reversed, the Ten of Wands may indicate a tendency towards laziness and the shirking of responsibilities.

The Ten of Cups

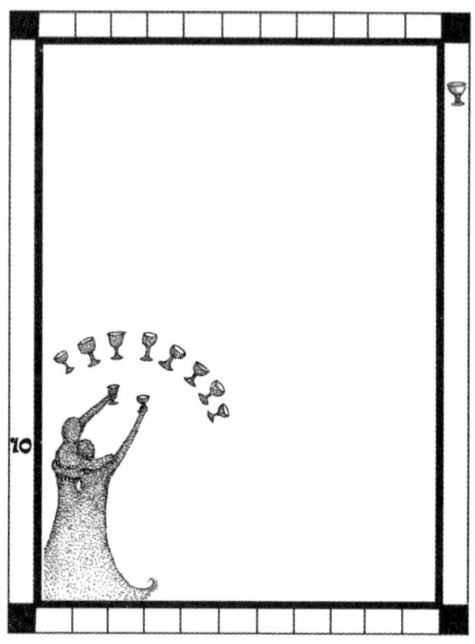

An embracing couple look up to a rainbow-like arc of eight cups, toasting them with a cup each. They seem joined, as if they have come together to form a unit. This is a happy conclusion to the emotional fairytale of the Cups suit, where there have been many joys and sorrows. From the ecstasy of first love and the kindling of friendships of the Two and Three of Cups, this suit passed into the depths of dissatisfaction and despair in the Four and Five. The Six of Cups reminded them of the good things in life, and then followed the realisation and power of choices in the next two cards. The Seven showed us the overwhelming and sometimes glamorous seduction of the world of personal choice opening up, and the Eight showed the empowerment achievable through making a difficult decision and sticking to it. The Nine taught us that dreams really can come true, and here we see the fruition of that idea in the Ten of Cups. In the image we see that the ten cups are separated into the eight that arch above the couple, and the two cups which they hold in their hands. Looking back at the journey, we can see that with the two cups of true love, they are toasting the lessons they have learnt and the hard decisions they have made, as in the Eight of Cups, which have brought them together and led them to happiness.

Divinatory Meaning

The Ten of Cups can almost always be interpreted as a good indication to a positive outcome or situation. Although it is a card which is primarily concerned with emotional well-being, it may of course appear in many different contexts. If the question of the reading is regarding material matters, then the Ten of Cups may indicate that the querent has found a career which not only supports them financially, but which makes them feel happy and fulfilled. It is also likely that their job enables them to have time with loved ones and family.

It almost goes without saying that this card is a very welcome sight in a reading about relationships! The Ten of Cups is the 'happy ever after' ending, full of love, sharing, and hope for the future. Of course, no one can guarantee the 'ever after' part, but as it stands at the moment, the situation is certainly happy. There is a sense that much has been endured which has brought this couple together, which has made their bond strong enough to stand the test of time. Having established individual identity and happiness in the preceding Nine of Cups, this is a card which speaks of family bonds and loyalty, and the joy that can be found in togetherness.

Spiritually, this card speaks of contentment and connectedness. Perhaps the querent has found someone or a group of people where they can share and be open about their spirituality. They have finally found a path to happiness, which is one of the most profound and difficult things to achieve.

When reversed, the situation may seem ideal on the surface, but the emotional reality is lacking. The querent has achieved everything that they thought they wanted, but it turns out not to be what they needed to truly nourish their soul.

The Ten of Swords

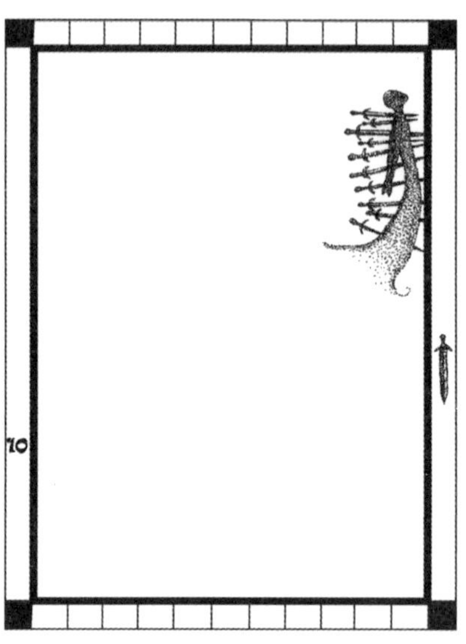

The bumpy ride of the suit of Swords reaches its alarming yet inevitable conclusion, as a figure is pinned to the side of the card, pierced by ten swords. Although this may seem a bleak image, comfort can be found in the fact that the long struggle is finally over. Although the Ace offers all the potential of clear thinking, logic, and communication, as soon as it splits into more than one line of thought, which is essentially what the swords represent, then trouble starts. With the Two was found an uneasy truce which resolved itself into sorrow. As soon as that has been healed with the healing and rest of the Four of Swords, the Five takes it all away again. An attempt at retreat follows in the Six, which is followed by sneakiness and deception. Soon the poor suit starts to fear its own shadow to the extent that it is afraid to even move in the Eight, and the nightmares brought into being by the Nine finally catch up with devastating consequences in the Ten of Swords. However, there is now nothing left to fear. The worst that could possibly happen has now really happened. Darkness has now been made solid and confronted, so can no longer offer the same threat and soon it will be time for a new dawn.

Divinatory Meaning

The Ten of Swords is not a card which is liable to make your average reader clap their hands with glee, but it does have valuable advice to offer. Essentially, on a surface level this card advises the querent that an idea or concept that they have been pursuing is going nowhere. It may have seemed promising, but energy would be best spent elsewhere, rather than flogging a dead horse. Obviously, it is not a very hopeful card to receive in regards to health matters, but due to its airy nature, it does tend to signify the deterioration of mental health rather than physical, though this is not always the case. It is a difficult stage to go through, but this card shows us the rock bottom which must sometimes be hit in order to bounce back up.

The Ten of Swords may well indicate the end of a relationship, if it appears in that context, or the realization that affection of a desired party is not shared. It is an important stage on the way to a more balanced existence.

Spiritually, this card may signify what is known as 'the dark night of the soul', when all seems hopeless, and connection to spirit seems distant. Part of this is often a loss of faith and a sense of loss of direction, but it will pass. Deeper understanding and a greater connection will often follow, just as it is always darkest before the dawn.

When reversed this card may signal the resurrection of an idea or way of thinking that had seemed dead. This may be either positive or negative, depending on the context and the combined cards. However, it may signal a state of being which will simply not pass when it really does need to, creating increased despair and despondency.

The Ten of Pentacles

A mature figure sits throned upon eight pentacles, wearing a ninth pentacle around their neck as a pendant or medal. Their robes seem to become the ground itself, on which a child stands lovingly by their side, holding the tenth pentacle in their hand. The suit of Pentacles has now finally brought all of the potential of the Ace into manifest physical form after a journey full of hard work, loss, gain, and patience. From the multitasking Two was found a skill that could

be developed in the Three. Afraid to lose what had been gained, enterprise gave way to miserliness in the Four of Pentacles. When the greedy Four became, (or perhaps beheld), the impoverished Five, they grew into the generous spirited Six, learning that wealth increases in value when it is shared. Through the Seven and Eight, the virtues of patience and hard work are learned. The fruits of these efforts can finally be enjoyed in the Nine, where comfort and independence are achieved. The result of this is someone who has the means to support a family, and a legacy to hand down, which is what we can see in the Ten of Pentacles.

Divinatory Meaning

In a similar fashion to the Ten of Cups, this is a card which speaks of unity and togetherness. Because of its earthy nature, the Ten of Pentacles tends to relate more to families and the establishment of a kingdom, no matter how big or small. If this card answers a question regarding career, then it may well be that the querent finds him or herself in a position of authority and influence, but with most of the hard work now behind. Perhaps they now own a company that employs many people, but they no longer need to work themselves. It could show a prosperous retirement, or sometimes indicates a generous inheritance. It is also a sign that physical health and the quality of life are good.

The emotional dimension of this card speaks of a strong sense of family and duty to descendants, as well as the contentment that comes from knowing that you no longer have to struggle to put food on the table. Conversely, this card has been known to indicate the finalization of a divorce, along with a reasonable financial settlement.

If it is a reading on spiritual matters, then the Ten of Pentacles may indicate a happy existence as part of an earth-based spirituality, with wisdom gained which may now be passed to others. It may even indicate being part of a community with strong beliefs in the power of nature and respect for the land.

When reversed, material gain brings no comfort, and may cause conflict within a family. Siblings squabbling over who is entitled to what inheritance would be one example of the Ten of Pentacles' reversed meaning, as would a complicated and painful divorce.

The Court Cards

There are 16 court cards in the Tarot, consisting of a King, Queen, Knight, and Page for each suit. It is immediately apparent upon looking at these cards that what sets them apart from the rest of the deck is their defined features and sense of personality. This is because, returning to our theatrical analogy, the courts cards are the characters of our play. When they appear in a reading, they usually indicate a person who is currently playing a part in our lives. One of the advantages of *The Transparent Tarot* is that through noting which cards appear combined with our court card, we can gain a clearer understanding of what part of our lives this individual may be involved in. The court cards can also stand for aspects of our own personality or modes of behaviour. They can sometimes even stand for events—like all of the cards, they are open to be interpreted by your intuition, and under that guidance, can mean almost anything!

Although the old titles of King, Queen, Knight, and Page may seem related to status, it is more accurate to relate them to age and gender, Kings and Queens being obviously more mature than Knights or Pages. A basic analysis of the personality type indicated can therefore be quickly and easily attained by looking at the nature of their suit and their level of maturity. For example, the King of

Cups is a mature man of an emotional nature. We can extend that to presume that with that maturity comes compassion, wisdom, and understanding, but sometimes deep sadness due to his sensitivity and the heartbreak he must have encountered in his life. Of course a King may not necessarily be physically male or indeed old—a young woman with these same qualities may be represented by this card also.

The Courts are designed so that when you have two or more of different rank within a combination, a family is formed. Because each of the courts is placed in the same position on the card as others in different suits but of the same rank, it can make for an interesting effect when two or more of the same rank are combined. When this occurs, you can choose to combine the traits of each like so:

This combination gives the impression of one individual who may have the qualities of both court cards within their personality, in this case, practical yet sensitive and compassionate.

For a different effect, you may prefer to flip or reverse one of them, like this:

This combination produces an impression of two individuals, but perhaps within the same situation. Another possibility is that one of the cards might be reversed, which tends to emphasise that character's darker character traits, or may even represent the shadow self of the upright card.

Of course there are many methods for you to experiment with! Remember you do not even need to be limited by the frame of the card. Try experimenting with more random placements and staggered overlaying, which there will be more about in the section entitled, *"How to use the cards"*.

When studying and using the court cards, try asking yourself some of these questions:

> What sort of person do I think this card shows?
> Do I like this person or not?
> What traits do I share with this person?
> Who do I know that is like this person?
> What can I learn from this person?
> What does this person have to say to me?
> Which card or combination of cards would I choose to
>   represent myself at this time?

The Kings

As has already been mentioned, the court cards can be read on many levels. On a surface level, the Kings represent mature men, possibly with some of the physical characteristics displayed on the card. On a deeper level, the Kings represent experienced people with wisdom and authority, who in reality may be of any age or gender. For those who are interested in the elemental subtleties of Tarot, the Kings carry the quality of the element of fire as well as the element of their suit. This gives them the qualities of drive, ambition, and charisma which make them natural leaders.

The King of Wands

This card shows an attractive and dynamic mature man, clothed in the red of his suit and confidently carrying a staff-like wand. The King of Wands is an intensely charismatic individual, and as such can be very charming. This does tend to mean that he is used to getting his own way, but his manner is so warm and personable that it is rarely an objectionable trait. He is active and passionate, and is likely to be involved in a direct way with championing worthy causes. The combination of his natural charisma and the wisdom of his experience means that he is someone that people really listen to when he talks, and would be an excellent public speaker or performer. He is not only inspired but inspirational to others, and has the energy to give enthusiastic support to projects. The King of Wands is a natural leader, particularly in spiritual or creative matters.

If the card appears reversed, then we lose many of the positive character traits, though he is sure to think he possesses them! The King of Wands reversed is a poor leader, who bullies others into obeying him. Whilst he may be charismatic, he is unashamedly shallow, and is far more likely to be concerned with selfish pursuits than good causes, unless he can see some way by which his image may gain from the involvement. His mood is governed by his temper, and he likely gets his own way not by charm, but by others fearing the consequences of disobeying him. At his worst, the King of Wands reversed can be a real tyrant.

Divinatory Meaning

When this card appears in a reading, it could indicate that a King of Wands type person is important or becoming important in the life of the querent. Of course it could also stand for the querent, or simply an aspect of their personality. The King of Wands could signify a phase of feeling dynamic and in control, possibly deservedly being the centre of attention. If he indicates a possible event rather than a person or character trait, then he may well herald a position of authority within an imaginative and flourishing company. Depending on the combined cards, he may indicate an assumption of more authority in spiritual matters, showing that there is no longer a need to defer to others. He may also indicate a career in politics, as power and leadership are strong aspects of his character.

Similar to the character description above, if the King of Wands is ill-aspected, he may signal a severe loss of temper and excessive anger and frustration in a situation. The King of Wands reversed could well mean the seizing of power by force, which has not been rightfully earned and will not be truly respected. He could point towards shallow motivations, such as the desire for fame or celebrity, which pushes more noble concerns to the background. In this aspect, the King of Wands shows that ego has become too important and life is losing its true substance.

The King of Cups

Here we see a fair-haired mature gentleman, robed in watery blue and holding out a golden cup. His hair is long, as if to show a relaxed attitude, or possibly simply that a smart appearance is not his top priority. The King of Cups has all the sensitivity and emotional depth of his suit, combined with maturity and experience. This is someone who has really seen the true value in the lessons that life has taught him, always taking time to feel things truly and deeply, whether joyous or sad. His experiences and understanding have led to a sense of genuine empathy with those around him, and this caring nature makes him a wonderful father. Even if he doesn't have a biological family of his own, he will be surrounded by those who see him as a father figure, and he will protect and care for them as his own.

He has an interest in artistic expression and spirituality through which he can explore the mysteries of the self and the universe. He will probably be attracted to ancient traditions and practices, and will have a passionate interest and knowledge of ancient history. His innate knowledge of things which may remain hidden to others gives him a sense of gentle inner strength and purpose.

His deeply sensitive nature means that he is suited to a gentle career, such as counseling, where he would be able to draw on his personal experiences to help others. He may also be drawn to archeology or art history, as he is fascinated by uncovering the mysteries of the past.

If the card appears reversed, then his depth of emotion is not extended in a caring way, as he is likely to be wallowing in self-pity. His many experiences of the world will not have been seen as valuable lessons, but rather as painful encounters which were hurled against him by an uncaring world. His sensitivity becomes over-sensitivity, and he may well suffer from depression and emotional imbalance.

Divinatory Meaning

When the King of Cups appears in a reading, it may mean that someone of that description or perhaps with some of those characteristics is playing a role in the life of the querent. If he is not representing a figure, however, he could indicate a phase of increased empathy with the suffering of the world, accompanied by the drive to do something about it. Perhaps the querent is being drawn towards working as a counselor or therapist, or perhaps conserving history is becoming increasingly important to them. The King of Cups can be a sign of increased emotional maturity and responsibility, sometimes indicating a man who is finally ready to propose or start a family. This card advises us to approach life with gentle understanding and to use our wisdom of experience to help others. He speaks of inter-connectedness and the oneness of being.

When reversed, this card may be a sign of emotional problems, particularly a tendency towards depression or emotional exhaustion. It is the card of someone who has seen too much and finds it difficult to deal with. The King of Cups in this aspect carries a burden of deep grief and uncontrolled sorrow, which can make him moody and unpredictable.

The King of Swords

In this image, we can see an older man, his brow furrowed from a life of deep thought. He wears purple robes and holds the symbol of air, the sword, in front of him. The sword represents the sharpness of the mind, and the ability to judge, both dominant qualities of the King of Swords. Although he is not emotionally cold, he does not allow his emotions to dictate his actions, but rather acts on logic and rational thought. He has a quick mind and enjoys a good debate and

he enjoys puzzles and intellectual games such as chess. His intelligence and detachment enable him to see both sides of an argument, but he will always fight for the side he believes to be right and just. This means that this card is often associated with those in the legal profession, particularly lawyers and judges. His keen mind would also be well suited to working with computers or accounting, when attention to detail is all important.

The King of Swords may also represent a scientist or a teacher of scientific subjects, although he is likely to have little patience for those who are slow to learn—he certainly has little tolerance for unintelligent people! Whilst in general preferring matters of the mind to that of spirit, he may well take an interest in the scientific research behind unexplained phenomenon if he felt there was justification. His curious and insightful mind is always ready for new challenges, but it is difficult to change his mind on a subject once it has been made up.

This stubbornness is a trait which is liable to come to the fore when this card is reversed. At his most ill-natured, the King of Swords is without honor, using his sharp intellect and will to manipulate others. He will do this sometimes for his own advantage, but often for the satisfaction that cruelty for its own sake provides him.

When reversed, his innate sense of justice is replaced by a purely egocentric system by which whatever he says goes, or else! He is all too ready to punish those who would dare to cross him, and is lacking in loyalty and emotional attachment. The King of Swords will allow nothing and no-one to get in the way of his pursuit of an idea, even if it is destructive.

Divinatory Meaning

If this card appears not to indicate an individual, the King of Swords may indicate an interest in scientific or legal matters. A career in law is traditionally indicated by this card, as well as the more obvious Major Arcana card, 'Justice'. Generally, unless reversed, this card would indicate that any legal matters are leaning in favor of the querent. He may also indicate the deepening of intellectual understanding of the world, perhaps a discovery of new scientific evidence which supports the querent's beliefs. On a very basic level, this card could indicate the ability to win a debate or argument.

When reversed, the argument is most likely lost. Legal cases may not find in favor of the querent, despite what might seem fair or just. This card could be an indicator of mental turmoil or a tendency towards cruelty, even towards the self. It could be that rather than a cruel individual in the querent's life, this card shows a general atmosphere of mental cruelty and abuse.

The King of Pentacles

In this card we see a dark-haired man with earth-toned skin, wearing green robes and gently yet securely holding a green pentacle before him. The King of Pentacles is practical yet passionate, strong yet gentle, and endlessly patient. He has a connection to the seasons and the cycles of earth, which makes him a natural farmer or gardener. As part of his love of nature, he has a natural way with animals and would also be suited to a career as a veterinarian. Creatively, he may be attracted to working with

clay, sculpture, and ceramics, or possibly even blacksmithing. As material matters are ruled by his suit, the King of Pentacles tends to be financially comfortable, particularly wishing to provide his family and loved ones with a secure environment in which to flourish. He is deeply caring and protective of his family and friends, though may find it difficult or unnecessary to express verbally. Despite this, no-one would be in any doubt that he cared for them, as he would express it in his actions and warm, generous manner. He is very loyal and immensely trustworthy.

Although he is quietly confident, he is not quick to make decisions, preferring to take time to choose the best course of action. However, once an action is decided, he is not afraid to put in any hard work necessary to implement it. Although practical of nature, the King of Pentacles may find spiritual inspiration from nature and the beauty of the world around him.

When reversed, the King of Pentacles can become acquisitive and stubborn. Instead of living in harmony with his environment, he exploits it, taking all he can for himself. The negative traits of the King of Pentacles are greed and materialism. This would be the sort of person who would gladly trample their brother for an opportunity to become head of the company, but would not wish to do the hard work when he got there, merely reaping the rewards.

Divinatory Meaning
When not representing an individual in a reading, the King of Pentacles may point towards a secure financial position and a comfortable lifestyle. He speaks of a respect for nature and love of all growing things. He could indicate a love of gardening, or a career in agriculture, animal care, or ecology. The home environment signaled by this card is warm, loving, and stable. This card is a sign that the querent has support and that they should not want or struggle for anything, and may be coming into more control of their financial situation. The King of Pentacles is also a sign of good health and diet, perhaps heralding a more organic and self-sufficient lifestyle.

If this card should be reversed in a reading, then connection with natural balance is being lost. It could indicate ill-health, possibly through poor diet and lack of exercise. The King of Pentacles reversed could be a sign of an over-materialistic attitude, or living in a materialistic atmosphere. He could also hint at gluttony or eating disorders.

The Queens

In the Queens, we see mature and confident women, but they can also indicate the feminine qualities in men, or the qualities of wisdom in the young. The Queens are connected to the inner mysteries of their element, and are intuitive and creative. They express the qualities of the element of water, which means they are natural empaths and healers.

The Queen of Wands

In this card, we see a striking and charismatic red-haired woman. She has an air of the dramatic about her, and is holding her wand confidently aloft. The Queen of Wands is vivacious and charming and has no problem in attracting and holding the attention of others. This natural spark, combined with an intensely creative nature and active imagination means that she is ideally suited to a career in performance. In theatre, she thrives as an actor, but would also be a wonderful director. However, she might find it difficult to repress the urge to play all the parts! She is also an expressive and powerful singer. Although she is quite a diva and enjoys the attention, she is equally supportive of others, and makes a wonderfully dynamic mother, encouraging her children to express themselves freely, but letting them know in no uncertain terms where the boundaries lie. She may seem unconventional, even eccentric, to others, but she is admired and even envied for her ability to be idiosyncratic and exuberant. This is rooted in her strong sense of self-confidence, which is unlikely to be compromised by the demands of others. She is likely to be independent, though sensual and loving in a relationship, and well traveled. She is quite a socialite, her energy is high and her laughter is contagious.

Of course when reversed, it is easy to imagine how tempestuous the Queen of Wands can become. When her negative qualities are highlighted, we see a self-important prima-donna who is not to be crossed. Her creative side is marred by a huge ego and a childish need to be the centre of attention, and she will use her charisma to ensure she always gets her own way. If that fails, then she will unleash her temper, which is a fearsome beast indeed!

Divinatory Meaning

When not indicating an individual, this card could herald a new period of independence and self-empowerment, particularly for women. There is a strong sensual aspect to her character, so she could signify an increased enjoyment of sex, perhaps finding ways to liven up a long-standing relationship. This card could also signal a career in theatre, or certainly something that involves socializing and dealing with the public. Perhaps she is simply stating that it is time to enjoy being the centre of attention for a while.

If reversed, then the Queen of Wands may be indicating a rather shallow need to be liked which manifests as embarrassing behavior in public and desperate gestures. This card reversed in a warning of the pitfalls of desiring fame and attention, suggesting that there are more important factors in life which must be put first.

The Queen of Cups

Here we see a dreamy looking woman with long, flowing fair hair, holding a golden cup before her. The Queen of Cups carries all the deepest qualities of the element of water. She is deeply sensitive and intuitive, using these skills to support and heal others. She is profoundly psychic in a natural and unassuming way, able to see below the surface of any person or event. Her essential nature is benevolent and full of compassion for her fellow beings. The Queen of Cups will always see the best in ev-

eryone, and try to show them those qualities in themselves. This talent of encouraging self-love and increasing other's feeling of worth and purpose means she is a talented healer, particularly of emotional problems. She is likely to be interested in alternative medicine and spiritual practices which suit her intuitive nature.

Although she may not always stand out in a crowd, she is well liked by most people for her gentle manner and caring ways. She is likely to be quite soft-spoken, but worth listening to, as she has great insights to share. In a relationship, she is deeply romantic and supportive of her partner, as well as being a wonderful mother. Family is important to the Queen of Cups, and as well as loving her own immediate family, she probably has quite a large extended family of close friends, as her strong sense of loyalty inspires that same equality in others.

When reversed, the Queen of Cups can become quite a dark character, full of doom-ridden premonitions and hurtful insights. If in her lighter aspect she can see the best in people, in this aspect she sees only the worst in them, and takes satisfaction from pointing out their shortcomings. She uses her emotional awareness to manipulate others, blackmailing them with threats of destructive and harmful behavior. Her moods are unpredictable and sometimes frightening, like a storm out at sea. She can reach the rock bottom of depression and drag all those close to her down with her.

Divinatory Meaning

If the Queen of Cups does not seem to represent an individual in your reading, then she could indicate a deepening expression of love and romance in a relationship.

She could also be the sign of an increase in the size of a family, (look for combinations with the Empress), or an increase in psychic ability and intuition, (particularly if combined with the High Priestess). Another possibility is that she could be advising seeking the help of a healer or alternative therapist, showing the cause of any health problems to be primarily emotional or spiritual.

If reversed, the Queen of Cups may warn against extreme mood swings, and a tendency towards emotional disorders. She could also be connected to the need for emotional escapism by artificial means, such as alcoholism or drug addiction. She also warns against disloyal actions such as infidelity and false prophecies. Intuitions may turn out to be just paranoia in disguise, and as such can prove harmful, particularly if acted upon.

The Queen of Swords

This card shows a severe yet beautiful woman, with a slightly oriental appearance and iron-gray hair swept back from her face, blowing in the wind. She holds the sword firm and straight before her. The Queen of Swords is an intellectual woman, with high principles and strong ideals. She likes to be able to rationalize all experiences and is likely to be extremely well-read in a wide range of subjects, sometimes even learning about something at great length in order to be able to dismiss it as unviable. She does not waste time on trivial chit-chat or niceties, and this can make her seem rather aloof and unapproachable. She has no patience for idiots, but has a deep respect for her intellectual equals and superiors. The best way of winning her friendship may well be to engage her in heated debate! She is a captivating and inspiring public speaker, as she is comfortable in the realm of words and ideas. She may well be suited to a career dealing with the mind, such as psychology or research and makes an excellent tutor or lecturer. When her passion is stirred by causes which she sees as just and deserving of her dedication, she is certainly a force to be reckoned with. Any prospective relationship must be with an intellectual equal, or it is unlikely to last, and she will always remain fiercely independent. Often she will reject emotional involvement altogether, preferring the realm of research and ideas and very often oblivious to any interest that is shown in her. She has a quick wit and a sharp tongue which she enjoys using, but may sometimes regret pushing people away. As a mother, she can appear distant, but will be very supportive of her children's intellectual development, making sure they have a stimulating education and are always open to new ideas. However, any problems are likely to be tackled from a purely logical and problem solving point of view, rather than with sensitivity or feeling.

This aspect is particularly emphasized when the Queen of Swords is reversed. Her negative aspects include an attitude of superiority coupled with the knowledge of what harm her words can do. At her worst, she can be wickedly manipulative and vindictive, bringing respected figures down with a few choice words. She can be deceptive, creating elaborate lies and fantasies in order to try and make herself look good and bring down opposition. She can become close-minded, convinced of her own righteousness even if she is proved wrong.

Divinatory Meaning

If not indicating a real person in the life of the querent, the Queen of Swords may signal a career in scholarly research, lecturing or a deepening of an intellectual pursuit. This card could be a sign of success in a public debate, or an increased awareness of psychology. Perhaps the querent is becoming more respected in an intellectual field, or is experiencing a time of increased mental clarity and expression of ideas.

When reversed, this Queen may be a sign of increasing coldness and emotional withdrawal. She could be warning of the dangers of harmful gossip, either indulging in it, or becoming the victim of it. This card reversed is an indicator that an over attachment to logic and rationality may have caused loneliness and detachment. This card may also indicate the loss of a debate due to a fundamental flaw in the argument or to some dishonesty behind the scenes.

The Queen of Pentacles

In this card we see an olive-skinned woman with long, healthy looking hair tied up in a practical plait. She is holding the green pentacle before her in a stable position. The Queen of Pentacles is a practical and charming character, with a deep connection to the earth and all growing things. She is very healthy, and has natural instincts regarding exercise and diet. This might lead her to a career in fitness or nutrition, and she might also be interested in herbal remedies and homeopathy. As pentacles are also connected to wealth, she has a good business sense, aided by her practical nature, which means she is unlikely to be short of money. If she does find herself on a low income, she will be able to make the best of it, and make a little go a long way. It is possible that she may run her own business, as well as being an excellent housekeeper.

The Queen of Pentacles is naturally domestic, and is likely to be very nurturing of both her partner and her children. Because of her good health sense, she also tends to be very physically attractive, albeit in an earthy way, and enjoys a sensual and fulfilling relationship. She can be quite old-fashioned in the home, often being quite happy to be the mistress of the kitchen and hearth. She is also fairly conventional in her style and appearance, putting practicality above glamour or imagination, but she still manages to make simple things look good. Despite her domestic and conventional leanings, she is very creative, and may excel at crafts and design. She most likely enjoys spending time in her garden, which will be full of interesting and beautiful plants, probably many of which she can use in her cooking or for home remedies. She is likely to grow her own vegetables, if she has the space, and take a keen interest in organic farming and sustainable living.

When reversed, the Queen of Pentacles can become conventional to the point of being dull, and practical to the point of being constricting. Material matters and beautiful things become her prime concern, and she has no understanding or tolerance of people who might wish to seek higher matters or express themselves in unusual ways. The Queen of Pentacles can be stubborn and stuck in her ways, and almost bigoted about anything which seems 'alternative'. She may well also be prone to over-indulgence in food, or possibly the opposite, becoming obsessed with her appearance to such an extent that it is damaging.

Divinatory Meaning

If the Queen of Pentacles does not seem to indicate an individual, she may indicate an interest in domestic or health matters. Perhaps the querent is entering a phase where they have decided to really look after their health, or spend more time at home with family. She also suggests good business decisions, and a stable, comfortable income. The Queen of Pentacles could also be heralding a shift into a more ecologically friendly and self-sufficient lifestyle.

If reversed, this card could signify ill-health and a poor diet. Whilst this could simply mean too much junk food, there is also a warning of possible eating disorders. The Queen of Pentacles reversed is a sign that material matters have become too important, and that there is too much attention being paid to surface appearances at the expense of more important concerns.

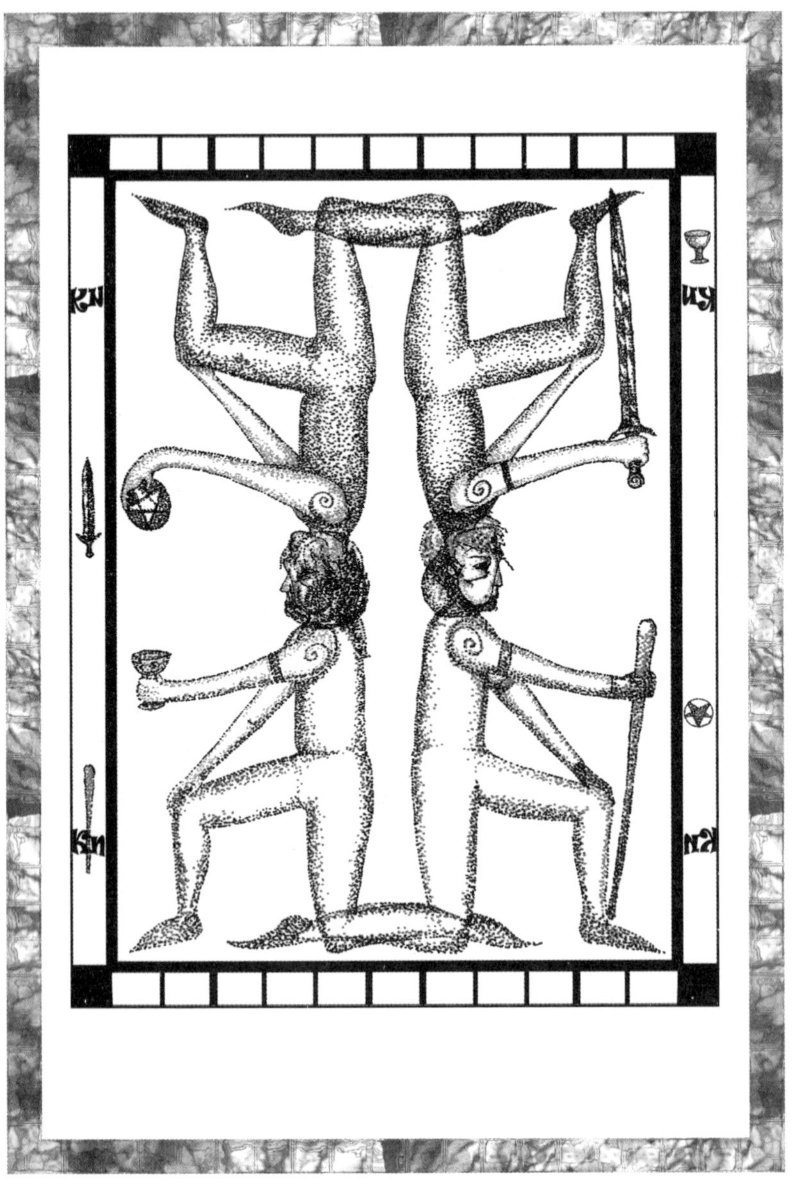

The Knights

The Knights represent young males, though may also stand for the qualities of drive and enthusiasm in people of any age or gender. They are connected to the realm of air, and hence have a keen intellect and interest in concepts and ideas. This leads to a love of travel and exploration, a sense of adventure, and an inspired imagination.

The Knight of Wands

Here we see a striking young man, with bold, red hair. He is kneeling, but ready for action, holding his wand out before him as if about to set off on a journey. The Knight of Wands is full of the energy of youth, with the drive and passion of fire, and the inspiration and intelligence of air. This makes him a very exciting character to be around, and he is likely to be very popular, with many friends and admirers. He has a keen sense of adventure and strong leadership qualities, which are borne out of natural charisma rather than experience. This may lead to many impetuous decisions and an ability to get not only himself, but others, into some very precarious situations. He is likely to excel at sports, particularly those which are unusual or involve an element of risk. He is also attracted to performance arts, being captivating to watch, and is likely to be an excellent dancer, on and off the stage! He has a strong urge to travel and see as much of the world as possible, which leads him to many encounters that most would not even dream of. His sense of adventure may also extend to spiritual matters, leading him to perhaps spend time with indigenous cultures or alternative groups, always immersing himself in the experience. Through his wide palette of worldly experience, he develops strong opinions and is passionate about political issues.

Coupled with his fearlessness, he is a powerful campaigner for just causes, likely to get involved in as active a way as possible.

The negative side of his character that may come to the fore when the card is reversed shows a young daredevil who takes too many risks, sometimes really endangering himself and others. This may well include driving far too fast and possibly under the influence of alcohol. He may even bully others into getting into trouble with him. If others warn him of danger, he simply laughs it off. The Knight of Wands reversed is simply out for as much fun as he can get, and certainly believes in burning the candle at both ends! He has little respect for any rules, and is likely to rebel purely for rebellion's sake. He may exploit his attractiveness to others by using them as he will, and may have several flings on the go at once. He relishes his reputation as being dark and dangerous. If he does become passionate about a political cause, then in his darkest aspect he may well be drawn to extremist groups and violence.

Divinatory Meaning

If this card does not indicate an individual in your reading, then it may be a sign of exploration and travel to exotic locations. The Knight of Wands in a reading gives a sense of adventure and spontaneity, perhaps encouraging the querent to jet off on a last-minute holiday, or even to set off around the world for a year! His influence can lead to many new and inspiring experiences, and to a renewed passion in life. He could indicate a career in sports or performance. Another possibility is that this card signals a new political or global cause which will stir the querent into decisive action, making them want to do what they can to make the world a better place.

When negatively aspected, the Knight of Wands may be warning against taking unnecessary risks or burning up too much energy. It could be time to slow down before someone gets hurt or in serious trouble. It could also be a sign of involvement in an unhealthy cause, or possibly being forced into dangerous action against your wish.

The Knight of Cups

In this card we see a sensitive-faced young man, with long fair hair tied back in a slightly disheveled ponytail. He holds out his cup before him, seemingly offering it to an invisible companion. The Knight of Cups is the archetypal romantic and chivalrous knight. He has a highly developed creative imagination and intensely emotional nature which means that he is often a talented musician, writer, or artist. He can be very broody, choosing his words carefully, but has a poetic and

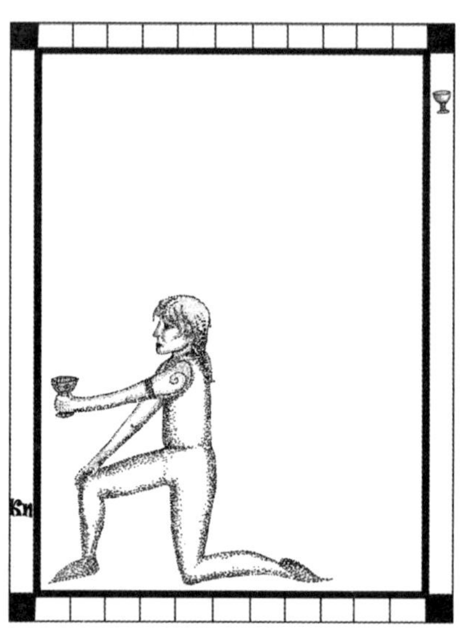

expressive manner when he chooses. He is very much in love with the idea of love, and has a tendency to put the object of his desire on a very high pedestal. When within a relationship, he is deeply loyal, but may sometimes overwhelm people with his depth of emotion and romantic gestures. The Knight of Cups offers himself completely to the object of his affection. He is not afraid of commitment, and is likely to propose early on in a relationship. Because he has such high expectations of love, he is often disappointed, but this heartbreak is a source of creative inspiration for him and very much a part of his character. He is also deeply spiritual, his life being a quest for universal truth, and this may lead to exploration of many faiths. When he finds his true path, his faith is very powerful.

When the Knight of Cups is reversed, his passionate nature can become quite unhinged. He may have several partners, but be convinced that he is deeply in love with all of them, causing confusion and indecision. He can be extremely moody and prone to bouts of quite self-destructive depression, lashing out at those close to him. He may suffer from a lack of self-confidence, not seeing the true talent and gifts that he has. In this aspect he has a tendency to spend long periods of time alone in the dark, dwelling on his misfortune and heartbreak. He feels that no-one could possibly understand his pain, as it is so deep, and refuses to seek comfort, to the extent that he actually seems to relish his own suffering.

Divinatory Meaning
One of the meanings that often emerges for this card when it is not indicating a person is that of a social invitation. The Knight of Cups may also indicate a romantic trip away, perhaps by water or on a cruise. He could simply be a sign that a romantic relationship is deepening and it could be time for a new level of commitment. Certainly this card often speaks of a love which will never be forgotten.

A career in the more introverted arts may be indicated, or simply that the querent is entering into a particularly poetic and creative phase. He could also signify an increased understanding and commitment to a spiritual path, or a quest for further knowledge and experience of such matters.

When this card is reversed, he may be a sign of painful romantic complications and heartbreak. He could indicate a period of dissatisfaction, broodiness, and depression. This card reversed could simply indicate a cancelled social event, or on a deeper level a broken engagement and lack of commitment. Loneliness and a masochistic indulgence in dark emotions are likely to be heralded by the reversed Knight of Cups.

The Knight of Swords

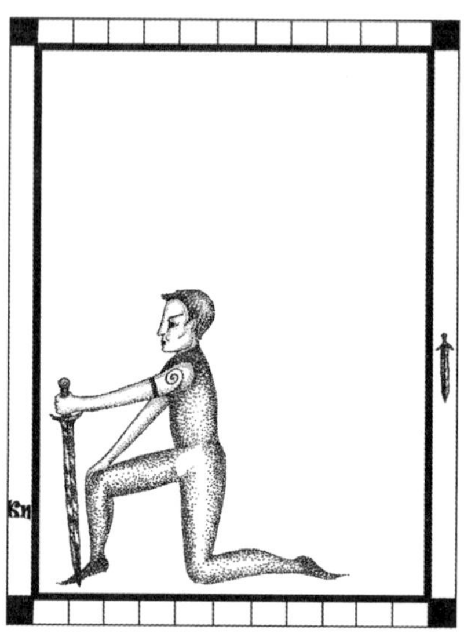

In this image, we see a young man with unconventional purple hair, holding his sword out decisively before him. The Knight of Swords lives in the realm of theories and ideas. He is extremely intelligent, and very aware of it, enjoying the fact that others may find him confounding and unpredictable. His enquiring mind and skills in communication might make him an excellent investigative journalist or detective, as he is always keen to find out what is happening under the surface. This drive to find out what makes things tick may also lead to an interest in the leading edge of science, particularly in areas such as quantum physics and chaos theory. He is fond of lively debate, and is quite capable of debating an intellectual viewpoint that he doesn't even personally hold, enjoying the challenge. He has many fresh new ideas, but not always the staying power to act on them, often flitting from one idea to the next. He may appear quirky and eccentric to others, but this can sometimes serve to inspire them to become more individual themselves. He enjoys socializing, but may not always listen to what companions have to say. He talks so much and so quickly himself, that others may find it very hard to get a word in! In social situations, he is a natural comedian, being quick witted and verbally dexterous. However, he may not always be sensitive to the feelings of others, freely identifying them as the subject of a joke if it means that he will get a laugh.

This aspect may be particularly emphasized when the Knight of Swords is reversed. His darker aspect is cold and vindictive, with a scathing wit which he has no qualms about unleashing on even the most undeserving victim. His awareness of his own intelligence combined with his youthfulness can make him extremely arrogant and unpleasant. Like many of the courts of his suit, when reversed he takes an unhealthy interest in spreading gossip and malicious rumors. He enjoys seeing the effect that this has, as it gives him a feeling of power over others. Another possible interpretation of this card reversed is the sort of person who has many ideas but never acts on them, living completely in his head and quite removed from practical reality.

Divinatory Meaning

When not indicating an individual, the Knight of Swords may speak of a thirst for knowledge of new and exciting subjects. He may be pointing to an enjoyable debate or exchange of ideas. This card is also sometimes a sign of traveling by plane, perhaps in search of inspiration and a fresh perspective. His sword cuts through any deception to find the underlying truth of a situation. He could signify a career or interest in journalism or even stand-up comedy.

When reversed, this card may warn against vindictive gossip and lies being circulated. The Knight of Swords reversed could also be a sign of loss of inspiration or the inability to manifest ideas. On a very mundane level, he can even signify delays to air travel plans. In his darkest aspect, this card could point towards serious psychological problems.

The Knight of Pentacles

Here we see a young, olive-skinned man, with practical short, dark hair. He seems to be admiring the pentacle he holds out before him. The Knight of Pentacles is a practical, down-to-earth sort of youth. He is trustworthy and steady, and though he tends not to stand out from the crowd, has a loyal nature which is appreciated by his friends. He is always honest and ready with common-sense advice, particularly on health or money matters. He likes to be comfortable and doesn't tend to stray too far from home, enjoying a familiar landscape and walks through his local countryside. Like other courts of his suit, he is very connected to the earth, and may be interested in geology and environmental studies. He would also be a very good doctor, nurse or vet. He has a natural way with animals, and may have many pets, often taking in strays or injured animals for a time. He tends not to be a great leader, preferring to work hard behind the scenes, and is uncomfortable in the spotlight. However, he provides the strong foundation that any project needs to succeed. He likes to be surrounded by beautiful things of high quality, and is willing to work hard to maintain that lifestyle. He is very happy

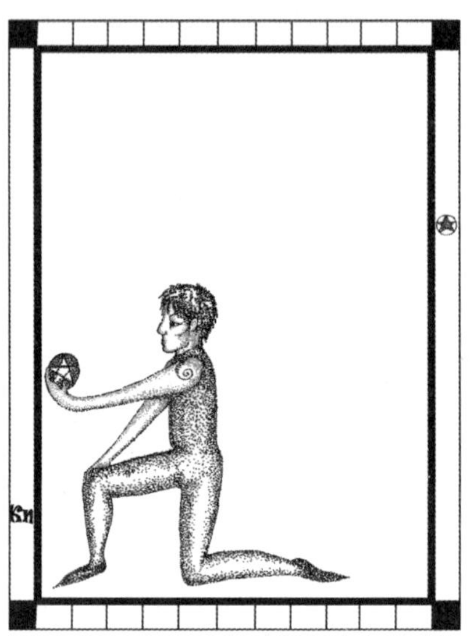

to share what he has with those he loves or others who are less fortunate. He does not require a high level of excitement and is not terribly romantic, but is a profoundly reliable and deeply caring partner.

When reversed, the Knight of Pentacles can become immensely dull, being so concerned with maintaining a state of stability and normality that he is dismissive of other possibilities. At his worst he can be immensely selfish, working for no goal other than personal material gain, exploiting the earth's resources without remorse or thought for the future. He may appear trustworthy, but in fact he will abuse this trust in order to further his own ambitions.

Divinatory Meaning

When not pointing to an individual, the Knight of Pentacles may indicate an increased awareness of environmental issues, and practical ways of living a more sustainable lifestyle. He is a sign of being sensible with money, and progressing slowly but steadily through a career. He may also indicate a journey across land or possibly a camping holiday.

When reversed, he warns against being too motivated by material concerns. The Knight of Pentacles reversed may also warn against betrayal by someone who seemed trustworthy. He is also a sign of lack of organizational skills and practical application. In his darkest aspect, this card speaks of the dangers of over-exploiting precious resources for selfish profit or pleasure.

The Pages

The Pages are pictured as young girls, but although they may represent children of either gender in a reading, they also may stand for qualities of potential, innocence and enthusiasm in others. They are connected to the element of earth, as well as that of their suit, which makes them rather like a seed of their suit's potential putting out its first roots and shoots into the world to share with others. Another detail which I have added in this deck is that the Pages have differing lengths of skirt. This is because it seemed to be that they grew in maturity of nature as they progressed from Wands through to Pentacles, so the longer skirt denotes the more 'grown up' attitude, within their natural youthfulness. When not representing people, Pages also traditionally stand for messages related to the area ruled by their suit.

The Page of Wands

Here we see a young red-haired girl hurrying off the edge of the card, carrying her wand like a new toy or prize from some adventure. The Page of Wands is a charming yet exhausting package of enthusiasm, energy, and adventurousness. She is likely to stand out from the crowd at a very early age, not only for her boundless energy and untempered charisma, but for her strong sense of individuality. The Page of Wands does her best to be at the cutting edge of fashion, but always in a unique and

quirky way, which she has the personality to carry off. This makes her something of a trend-setter amongst her peers, many of whom will wish they had the courage to try something so different. She thrives in the spotlight, as she absolutely loves being the centre of attention. This means favorite subjects are likely to include sports, gymnastics, and theatre. She is a courageous child, and will probably be the first to volunteer for any new activity. She is highly sociable and popular, always keen to meet new people, and certainly not clingy or shy! She is an exciting friend, as she always thinks of inventive and fun games, but sometimes she can go a little too far.

This Page not only has incredible self-confidence, as she has not yet had any reason to doubt herself, but also immense reserves of will power, which means she can be a joy as long as things are going her way, but when they are not, she can be a terror!

When reversed, the Page of Wands becomes very challenging and almost unmanageable. Although she does have high energy, this is mostly channeled into not only causing trouble, but getting others into trouble. She rebels against all authority, even if it means sometimes missing out on things she might enjoy, and is always coming up with practical jokes to play on people which can sometimes turn nasty. In search of fun and excitement, she may encourage others into reckless and dangerous activities. She is flighty, with little staying power, and may suffer from attention disorders and lack of concentration. This causes her high levels of frustration, and she has a nasty temper, prone to tantrums even at an age when she shouldn't really be having them. At her worst, she may even become the playground bully, exerting her will over others and making sure that she always gets her own way.

Divinatory Meaning

If the Page of Wands does not seem to denote an individual within a reading, then she may be a sign of a new exciting adventure. This could be a course in an unusual subject, or one which involves courage and high energy. A good example of this might be a workshop in circus skills or contemporary dance. This card may indicate an atmosphere of enthusiasm and a new lease of life. The page of wands can also signify an important piece of news, an opportunity or a message which must be acted upon.

When reversed, the Page of Wands can point to a lack of staying power, for instance, the lack of ability to commit or concentrate on a task. She can also indicate sudden loss of energy, or a lack of ability to enjoy life. This card may appear reversed when new ventures are blocked or important messages are either not sent or are delayed.

The Page of Cups

In this card, a young girl with long, fair hair is running to the right of the card, perhaps to show someone the cup she carries, or its contents. The Page of Cups is sweet and sensitive, with a tendency to drift off into daydreams. Although she may seem a little shy, her heart is open and she has a caring and generous nature. She is deeply affected by her environment and things which are said or happen to her, to an extent which may seem strange to others. She is likely to take something which may have been meant as a passing comment or light-hearted joke very seriously, dwelling on it in silence for a long time after the person who actually said it has forgotten all about it. The Page of Cups is usually profoundly artistic and imaginative, expressing her dreams and emotions through her creations. She is often also highly spiritual, being very sensitive to otherworldly forces. Even as a young child she is fascinated by old buildings and stories of the past, giving the impression of having lived before. Therefore her favorite subjects are likely to be art, history, and creative writing.

She may not have many friends, as she tends to be a little withdrawn and introspective, but she will have a circle of very close friends whom she loves dearly and who love her in return.

When she sees a problem, she does her best to make it right, and always considers the feelings of others, including animals. Unfortunately, because of her sensitive nature, she is often the victim of bullying, as she finds it hard to contain her emotions, giving cruel bullies just the response they want.

If the Page of Cups should appear reversed, she is over-sensitive and high maintenance, finding it difficult to live in the real world at all. Her over-active imagination and tendency to daydream may manifest as exaggeration and lies, simply because she finds it genuinely difficult to tell fantasy from reality. If this trait does not find a creative outlet, then she may spiral out of control, at her worst becoming involved in escapist drug taking.

Divinatory Meaning

If the Page of Cups does not represent a person in a reading, she may be a sign of a new phase of artistic creativity. Perhaps a course in fine art or creative writing may be indicated, or a new interest in history. Her open heart and emotional nature mean that she can be a sign of a new romantic interest or relationship. She can also speak of the need for nurturing young children, the emotionally sensitive, or indeed our own inner child. As the Page of Cups is so aware of dreams and a deeper level of existence, this card may also be a sign of an awakening of spirituality, either through a course or through a natural process. She may also herald news regarding emotional ties or family, or even a message from the spirit world.

If the Page of Cups appears reversed in a reading, she could signal some bad news regarding a relationship or family. Perhaps a promising new relationship is broken off before it has even properly begun. Dreams are overturned, and a tendency towards escapist behaviour and depression may be indicated.

The Page of Swords

Here we see a young girl with an elaborate yet tidy hairstyle, carrying a small sword to the edge of the card, no doubt to tell someone all about what it is, where it came from, and how she came into possession of it. The Page of Swords is a highly intelligent, perhaps even precocious individual, with a love of analysis, logic, and communication. Not only does she have a quest and a talent for finding out how things work and why, but she also feels the need to share her understanding with others. If she finds an area which she does not yet understand, she will not hesitate to interrogate everyone she knows at length, until she finds satisfactory answers. She does, however, usually ask highly intelligent and insightful questions, and can communicate her knowledge to others clearly once it is acquired. This leads her to an enthusiastic interest in science, math, psychology, and philosophy, reveling in the chance to discuss concepts, ideas, and theories at length. This makes her a natural inventor.

She is a keen student, and may surprise her teachers with her level of knowledge and insight for one so young. Her drive to communicate, coupled with her youthful nature, can make her a bit of a chatterbox and she is the type to always say what she really thinks, with little regard for the consequences. This can mean she will often get into arguments, which she rather enjoys, as she tends to win. However, her quick wit and intelligence makes her a natural comic, and this will attract friends.

When reversed, the Page of Swords becomes a rather spiteful gossip, seeing her own intelligence as making her superior to others. She uses her logic and rational mind to demonstrate the flaws in others thinking, and laughs openly at those who have a more intuitive approach to life. She is capable of making very hurtful comments, often behind the back of those she is talking about. The Page of Swords reversed seeks popularity by putting others down and making them the object of ridicule. At her worst she can be thoroughly deceptive and cunning, making her an excellent spy.

Divinatory Meaning

When the Page of Swords does not indicate an individual within a reading, she may stand for a new course of study in the sciences or matters of the mind. This card may simply indicate a new intellectual insight, or inspiration for a revolutionary new idea or invention. This card may also indicate a message regarding development of a new concept or a scientific breakthrough.

The flip side of the Page of Swords is that she can be the sign of a breakdown in communication. She may also warn of malicious gossip and deceitful intentions.

The Page of Pentacles

Pictured in this card is a young dark-haired girl, proudly hurrying to show off her pentacle, which is probably well-earned payment for a job. The Page of Pentacles is the most practically minded of the Pages, and may seem rather old before her time. She is no-nonsense and down to earth, but also deeply caring, and though she doesn't particularly stand out in a crowd, she attracts friends through her trustworthiness and dependability. The Page of Pentacles can always be relied on to lend a hand, and is likely to earn extra pocket money at an early age by helping with domestic tasks. She is unusually tidy and well organised at a young age, and others may well chide her for her lack of a sense of fun and adventure. In fact, she's likely to be the voice of common sense in the playground or classroom, always pointing out the potential hazards and dangers to others. Although this may make her a little predictable, she has a pleasant personality and rarely gets into trouble. She is a hardworking and diligent student, and though she works

hard even at subjects in which she does not naturally excel, her favourite activities are likely to be crafts such as woodworking and pottery, and subjects connected to the earth such as geography, biology, and home economics.

She enjoys making things, and has a great deal of skill and patience, taking great care over her work and paying close attention to detail. This Page has a strong business sense and probably has savings put away from an early age, not being one for spontaneous splurges.

When reversed, the Page of Pentacles can be rather dull, always criticising others for their lack of diligence and taking little interest in anything spontaneous or fun. Her negative side is an unhealthy materialism, being motivated by monetary gain even at a young age.

Divinatory Meaning

If the Page of Pentacles does not stand for an individual in a reading, she may be a sign of a new business venture or money-making opportunity. She could also denote a period of study, perhaps of accountancy or business management, or something more creative, like a hands-on craft. She may denote a period of enjoying and appreciating the home environment and learning new domestic skills. She may also carry news of good fortune or a profitable job opportunity.

When reversed, her presence implies a downturn in fortune, and poor management of finances and domestic issues.

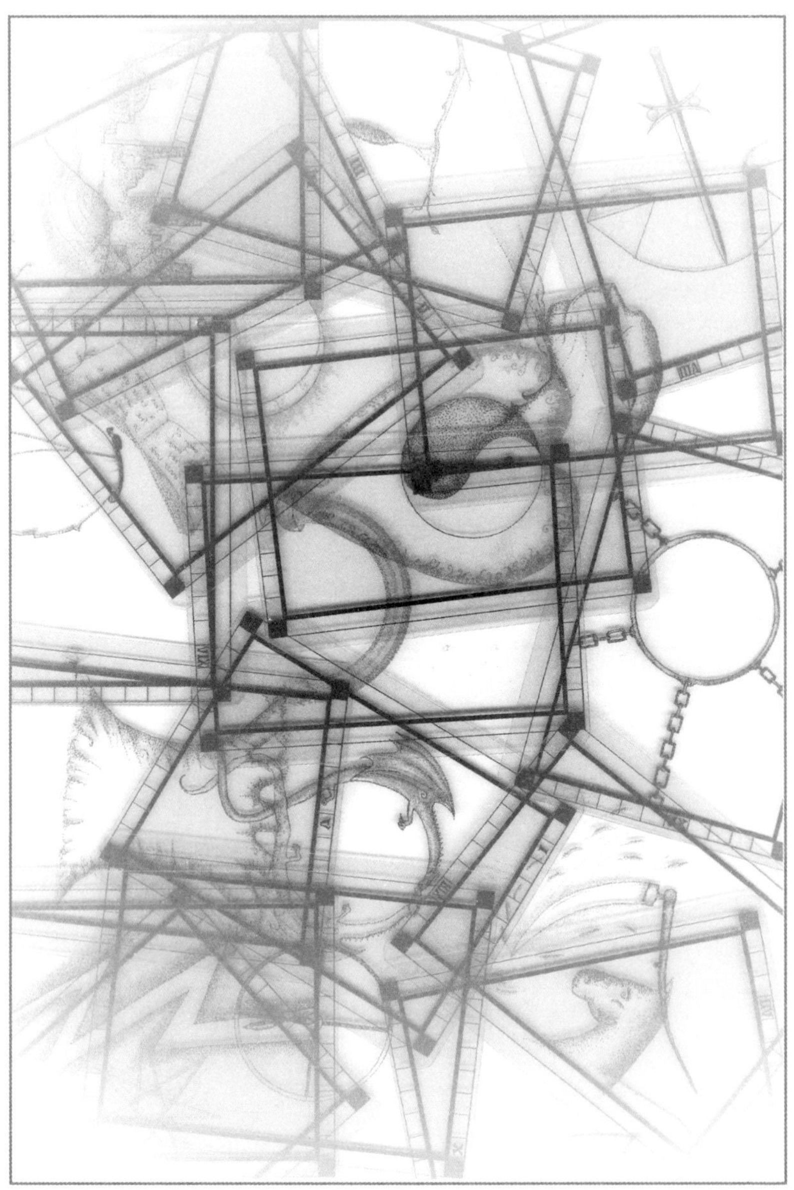

Chapter Three
HOW TO USE THE CARDS

Hopefully you will already have spent some time playing with and getting to know the cards. You may have even uncovered some ways of using them yourself already! Please don't think anything you might have thought of is wrong if it is not suggested in the book. *The Transparent Tarot* has so many possible uses and applications that I couldn't even possibly conceive of them all, let alone write them down. Instead, I have compiled a few suggestions to get you started, which hopefully you will adapt and use in ways that suit you. The following suggestions are designed to engage your imagination and hopefully inspire you to develop your own creative techniques for using the cards.

Divination

Divination is the most popular use for Tarot in modern times, providing us with advice and suggestions on how to deal with patterns and events that may arise and a mirror into our inner landscape. Whether you believe that divination puts us in direct contact with spirit, the collective consciousness of the planet, or whether it simply allows us access to the knowledge and awareness of surrounding patterns which are locked in our subconscious, the truth is that the process really can have many benefits, provided we approach it in the right way.

Focusing the question

One of the factors that is highly important if you wish to get an accurate answer to a question, is to be as simple yet as specific with the question as you can. Of course it's perfectly fine to do a reading which asks for general guidance, or to ask the cards to tell you whatever it is you need to know at this time, (a useful exercise, as we may not always consciously be aware of what we *need* to know!), but if there is a particular issue you wish to be answered, then phrase your question carefully in your head before you shuffle the cards. Remember, what we *want* may not necessarily be what we *need*, and the cards are a tool to help our inner selves find balance and guidance. For example the question, "How can I make Harold fall in love with me?" is unlikely to produce a useful response, whereas "What is the nature of the relationship between Harold and I?" or the more open, "What can I do to find love?" may be more insightful. A logical step in this process is creating your own Tarot spreads to cover specific questions within the same subject, such as "What can I do?", "What signs should I look for?", "What needs to change?" and so on. Think about the essence of the question, and create positions in your spread to cover the areas for which you need answers or guidance. If possible, the shape of the spread should reflect the nature of the question. For example, a card or combination which shows what is blocking you from achieving a goal may appear as a barrier between your significator and the card which indicates the goal itself.

Shuffling the cards

Shuffling the cards is an important part of the process, however you wish to use the cards, as it not only randomises them, but it infuses them with your energy, bonding them to you. Before you start using your cards for readings, make sure you give them a really good, long shuffle, thinking about how you would like the deck to help you in your life.

When you are going to use the cards in Divination, always shuffle beforehand, keeping the question or matter on which you wish to seek guidance clear and focused in your head. If it helps, you can sing a little song or make up a little 'shuffling chant'—whatever works for you. If you wish to use reversals, you may wish at some point to cut the deck into a few sections, turn a section round and then put the deck back together and carry on shuffling. If you wish, you may even flip a few cards sideways, (something simply not possible in other decks), and decide on your own interpretations for that occurrence, but others may find that a bit too confusing.

Some readers cut the deck into three sections and rearrange them when they have finished shuffling. You may prefer to simply spread the cards out and mix them around until you're happy that they're shuffled. You will find your own way. So long as you respect your cards, and remember to thank them, (and your guides, if you believe in spirit), then they will serve you well, whatever your methods.

When reading for others, ask them to focus on the matter they need guidance on and if you are comfortable with others handling your cards, give them the deck to shuffle. If not, ask them for their name and their question, and focus on these yourself as you shuffle.

Here are a few different techniques you might like to try…

The Card(s) of the Day

Something many users of Tarot choose to do, from the highly experienced to those who have just bought their first deck, is to draw a card for the day. At the beginning of the day, a single card is drawn from the deck which gives you an idea of what to expect from your day to come. Also, if you have a specific question, you may choose to ask the cards to give a simple response.

With *The Transparent Tarot*, shuffle your deck and then draw *three* cards, combining them as below.

Here we have the Two of Wands combined with the Sun and the Queen of Cups, which may indicate an empathic sharing and deepening of understanding, (Queen of Cups), between two dynamic individuals or viewpoints, (Two of Wands), leading to creative success and happiness, (The Sun).
These three cards can be interpreted as a single image, giving you a more detailed answer than is possible in a single conventional card. You may wish to add significance to which card falls in which layer, for example factors in the background might be on the lowest layer, or you may wish to keep it simple, it's up to you.

Thinking Outside the Box

Now that you've got your three cards, why not try combining them in different ways, or expanding on what you have? There is no need to be limited to keeping the image within its borders—why not let it loose?

Here, you can see the same three cards spread out into a 'filmstrip' arrangement, one of the many possible unique ways these cards can be used. Perhaps this could show a progression from past, through the present and into the near future, or perhaps it could show two individuals on either side and their common ground where they meet in the center. The possibilities even within this simple arrangement are almost endless. One possible method of expanding this spread is like so:

Here another two cards, (the Magician above, and the Nine of Cups below), have been added to make a cross shape. One possible use for this shape would be to use the central card as a significator, (indicating the querent at the time of the reading), and interpreting the four branches of the cross as the four directions and their corresponding elements. For example, the card above signifies North, and the element of earth. This card would show what is happening around the querent in terms of finances and health. As with all the cards, look at how it overlaps and interrelates with the central card.

So a brief interpretation of this spread might go something like this:

The querent, (represented by the central Two of Wands), is part of a new creative partnership which needs to choose its direction. They care deeply about this situation, and are able to empathize with the other party and their opinions, (Queen of Cups in the West, for water and emotions). While the querent brings this sensitive and creative side, the other party brings an idea with the potential for great success, (The Sun in the East, for air and ideas/thoughts/communication). Look at how these two cards interconnect with the central Two of Wands, and we can see that they flow nicely into, and complement the figures, showing how these two forces are natural parts of the two sides at work in the central card.

In the North, we have the Magician, which seems to interweave with the Two of Wands, showing that each side brings valuable qualities together in balance, and they have everything they need to make this project a commercial success.

Slightly disconnected from the other images, we see the Nine of Cups in the South, (Fire and the will/spirit), showing that this may bring the querent's dearest wish into reality, but its lack of interconnectedness with the other cards may mean that it seems too far off yet to really believe.

So, there we can see how a simple spread like this can give a clear and insightful reading.

The Three Position Spread

Something that is often used with traditional decks is the three card spread. These positions can be used to indicate past, present, and future; goal, obstacle, and outcome; or any number of different things, depending on what you need to know. I often use this simple spread to ask for a **gift**, a **challenge,** and a **goal** for my day. Instead of using three cards, with *The Transparent Tarot*, we can use three cards in each position in order to garner more detail, like so:

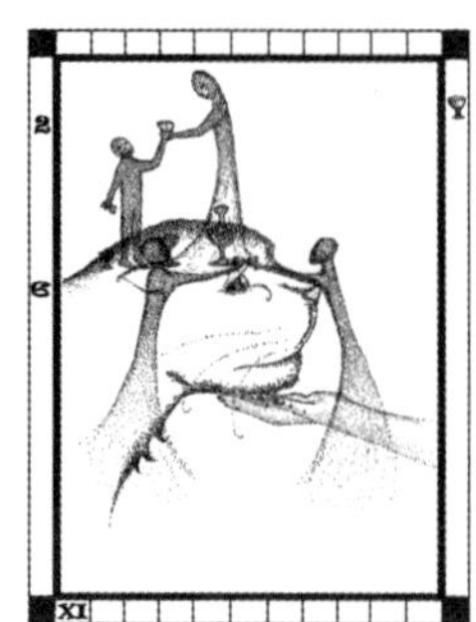

Thus, the cards in the first position, (the gift), may be interpreted as taking time to enjoy the blessings of motherhood, (the Empress), within a strong emotional unit, (the Ten of Cups), where you have the freedom to explore your dreams and magickal potential, (the Moon). If our original three cards from our first reading now take the position of 'the challenge' for the day, then they could be interpreted as meaning that there may be conflict indicated by the Two of Wands, which can be resolved successfully, (the Sun), by using a sensitive and caring approach, (The Queen of Cups). The combined image in the 'goal' position can be seen as advising finding the strength to deal with difficulties, (Strength), through fond memories, (the Six of Cups), of a loving relationship, (the Two of Cups).

Of course this is only one of many possible interpretations, but it shows that readings do not need always to be lengthy and complicated to be helpful.

You may choose to expand upon the central image of three cards with a filmstrip, like this:

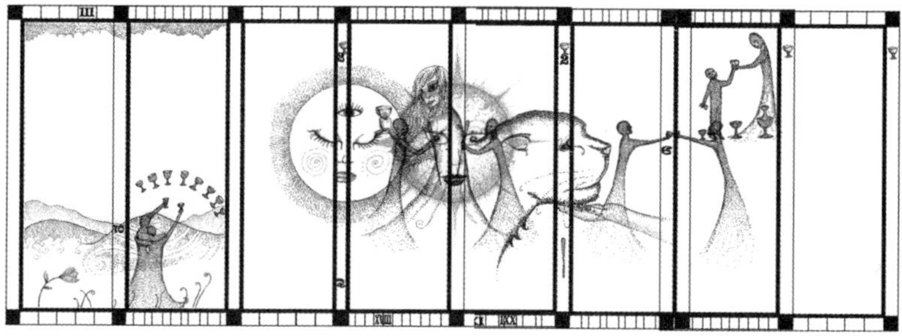

When melded together in this sort of flowing landscape, the cards may tell a different story, or add detail to that which has already been gleaned. For example, look at how the head of one of the figures of the Two of Cups becomes the child of the Six of Cups—what might this mean?

The (good old) Celtic Cross Spread

Experienced readers will all be very familiar with this spread as it is not only featured in most Tarot books, but is also used as a standard spread to get a good idea of the general atmosphere and events which surround the querent. Most Tarot users develop their own version of this spread, and this is my own personal take on the standard Celtic Cross:

Standard Celtic Cross spread

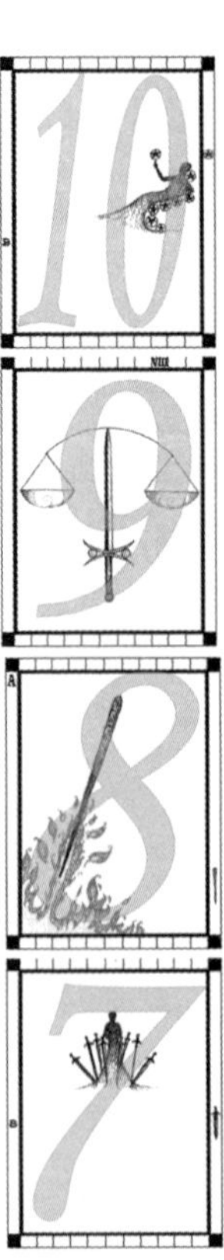

As you can see, there are two sections to this reading. On the left is the cross, which has two cards in the centre, (which obviously in the case of *The Transparent Tarot* can be seen as one image. These two cards are the significator, (Queen of Pentacles in this case), which represents the querent and may be consciously selected from the pack if you so choose, and their current circumstance, (Eight of Cups). Then, in order of placement we have the Underworld, (The Chariot), which shows factors which may remain unseen but are influencing events, and the Upperworld, (The Star), which shows the factor of destiny and spiritual guiding forces which may be at work. The position to the left indicates recent past, (the Seven of Wands) and to the right we have the near future, (the Knight of Cups). The section to the right of the cross is a simple line of four cards, which runs from bottom to top. The seventh card, (which is the first of this section), represents how the querent views themselves, (the Eight of Swords), followed by how they are viewed by those around them, (the Ace of Wands). Then we have the hopes or fears of the querent, (Justice), with the most likely conclusion being shown in the final card, (the Nine of Pentacles).

But rather than interpreting this standard reading, let's use *The Transparent Tarot* to its full advantage, and **add another two layers to this!**

Triple layered Celtic Cross spread

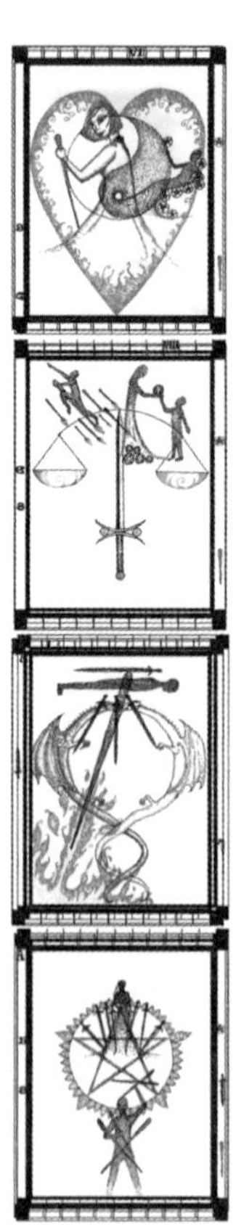

The following may give you some idea about how combinations work within a spread, and how to interpret them. Lay the cards in one layer first, then add the second layer for each position, and then the third, or which ever way works best for you.

Positions 1 and 2: **Significator and Situation.**

(The Queen of Pentacles combines with the Eight of Cups.) This image shows us that the querent is a well grounded and practical woman, and is materially comfortable. The presence of the Eight of Cups shows us, though, that the material is not enough, and she longs to leave her old life behind, willing to make sacrifices to reach for more spiritual and emotional fulfillment. Looking at this combination in more depth, perhaps the fact that she is facing *away* from the Eight of Cups shows that she is fighting this urge, or is in denial about her emotional needs.

Position 3: **Underworld.**

(The Page of Cups, The Chariot, and the Five of Swords reversed). So, under the surface we see that two opposing aspects of the querent's life are coming together and taking her towards where she needs to be. The reversed Five of Swords shows that she may feel guilty about the victory, as it is at someone else's expense. The Page of Swords emerging cup in hand shows that not only did she act from honest emotions, but that a budding new potential romance could emerge. Perhaps the new emotional depth she seeks?

Position 4: **Upperworld.**

(The Star, Death, and the Nine of Cups). Two Major Arcana cards here, shows that this is a strongly aspected position in her reading. Spiritually, she is being guided towards a new phase, leaving the old behind. The Star shines the light of inner beauty and expression on the harvest that is wrought by Death's scythe. Combined with the wish-fulfilling Nine of Cups, this shows that it is time for her to find her true self and purpose.

Position 5: **Recent Past.**

(The Fool reversed, the Seven of Wands, and the Two of Pentacles). The reversal of the Fool combined with the other two cards shows that while she might be successful in juggling many tasks despite excessive opposition, the responsibility of her work has meant that she has been unable to act spontaneously, and may feel as though she has missed more enjoyable opportunities as a result. These events will have highlighted her desire for more freedom of expression, representing something of a 'last straw'.

Position 6: **Near Future.**

(The Knight of Cups, the High Priestess, and the Four of Wands.) The Knight of Cups is facing her, showing that she may be about to receive a social or even romantic invitation, if she trusts the intuition shown in the High Priestess. This could lead to foundations for a more stable and creative future, hinted at in the Four of Wands.

Position 7: **How She Sees Herself.**

(The Five of Wands, the Ace of Pentacles, and the Eight of Swords.) The positioning here says a lot. The Eight of Swords within the Ace shows that she feels trapped by her material needs. The Five of Wands beneath, shows that despite being uncomfortable in her lifestyle, she struggles to support it.

Position 8: **How Others See Her.**

(The Magician, the Ace of Wands, and the Four of Swords reversed.) The Magician and Ace of Wands show that people see her as an incredibly energetic person, who really makes things happen. The Four of Swords reversed may imply that it appears she never needs rest, but look at how the tip of the Ace of Wands pierces the centre of the figure—perhaps they secretly worry about the damage her seemingly miraculous over-exertion is doing to her.

Position 9: **Hopes and fears.**

(Justice, the Eight of Wands, and the Six of Pentacles.) This image shows that she wishes to bring her life into balance, still being as active and driven as the Eight of Wands, but using that energy to do good work in the community, or for charity, as shown by the Six of Pentacles. The scales of Justice balance the two factors perfectly, and may even indicate that her all-consuming career is concerned with the legal system or rights in some way.

Position 10: **Most Likely Outcome.**

(The Lovers, the Queen of Wands, and the Nine of Pentacles.) The querent has gone through a transformation, (which was hinted at earlier in the Death card), and is now the Queen of Wands. This is likely to be closer to her true self. The Nine of Pentacles shows her taking the time to relax for once, and enjoy her new life. She is surrounded by the Lovers card, showing she has new priorities, and possibly a new relationship. Certainly she is more self-assured, so will be more attractive to others. The Queen and the Nine both sit comfortably within the heart of the Lovers, showing that she has reached a point of integration and balance within herself.

Other Uses for the Cards

Meditation and Magick

You may wish to meditate on certain cards and combinations in order not only to get to know the cards inside out, but to get to know yourself inside out! Using the Tarot in meditation can aid you in unlocking knowledge you didn't know you had, and in accessing your higher self. You may wish to consciously select cards for this process, or allow them to be randomly chosen, as in your card/s of the day. You might like to choose a combination which you think portrays your true self, or you may wish to create a combination which evokes qualities that you find more challenging. This could help you to face and integrate your shadow-self, or understand the perspective of others. There are many possibilities for you to experiment with, all with different lessons to teach. *The Transparent Tarot* offers you the ability to create your own images, beyond Tarot's standard seventy-eight.

When you have your card or combination of cards ready, find a time when you will be free and uninterrupted for around fifteen or twenty minutes, or how ever long is needed for your purposes. Dim the lights if you can, and sit comfortably and well supported with the image before you. Take some deep breaths and relax. With each breath out, let your worries and other nagging thoughts leave you. You may wish to imagine putting them in a box if you wish to return to them later, or dropping them down a well. If you do have a lightbox, illuminating the cards from beneath or behind may help you to focus more clearly. Study the image before you, clearing your mind of the concerns of the day. Allow the image to fill your mind, and try to hold it in your mind's eye as you close your eyes. When you can visualize the image clearly with your eyes closed, keep your eyes closed and focus on the image in your mind's eye. Keep your breaths slow and steady, and with each breath in, visualize a light behind the image, illuminating it, growing brighter. As you breathe out, imagine that light coming into your body through your forehead. With each breath, the image becomes brighter, its energy flowing into you with the light until you are illuminated with the light of the image from top to toe. Think about how every sense experiences this sensation, and try to remember any messages you receive. When you are ready, let the light slowly recede with each breath, until you are left once more with simply the image before you and the light behind it. Take time to recover your senses, opening your eyes to the physical world. It is wise to have a glass of water handy to have a drink afterwards, to make sure you are grounded, and a notebook, so that you can record your experience. So often even very vivid meditations can fade quickly in the memory, like a dream, but they may have important insights that making notes will help you to remember. It is also nice to look back on them after more work, as you will spot correspondences and confirmations which may otherwise have been lost.

Those who already use Tarot for ritual magick and other experienced magicians will be able to see the potential this deck offers. Combining images in the simple but potent way offered in *The Transparent Tarot* can create powerful and effective sigils on which to focus. A simple idea which anyone can do is choose a combination which reflects the energy that you want to bring into your life, and place it on your altar or a place of significance, (where it won't be disturbed), around the home. For example, a woman wishing to have a child may combine The Empress, the Six of Cups, and the Queen of Cups. Someone seeking a new job might choose the Sun, the Six of Wands, and the Ace of Pentacles. The image should be a balanced and aesthetic combination, with not too much confusion as the cards overlap. You may wish to light a candle by it, burn incense, or some other means of giving it focus and attention for a short time each day. This simple exercise will help to draw the energies of the image into your life.

Brainstorming

Brainstorming is the process of trying to bypass the stodgy rational mind, which can sometimes block inspiration, and come up with as many solutions or ideas as possible in a short amount of time, no matter how silly. It is a technique which can benefit everyone, from businessmen looking for new approaches, to writers looking for characters and stories, to artists looking for new inspiration, to just a simple person stuck in a rut who is looking for fresh ideas on what to do in life.

The Tarot, with its evocative seventy-eight images, is a great tool for brainstorming, provoking responses and ideas that would not otherwise surface. Well, imagine the possibilities of using *The Transparent Tarot*, which can produce an almost infinite array of images! Either by drawing cards at random, or by using the whole deck at once and seeing what different images emerge, or by many other methods, the resulting images will be a great source of inspiration and ideas.

Here is a spread which was designed with brainstorming in mind, but which also has many other applications.

Ripples of Consequence/Wheel of the Year Spread

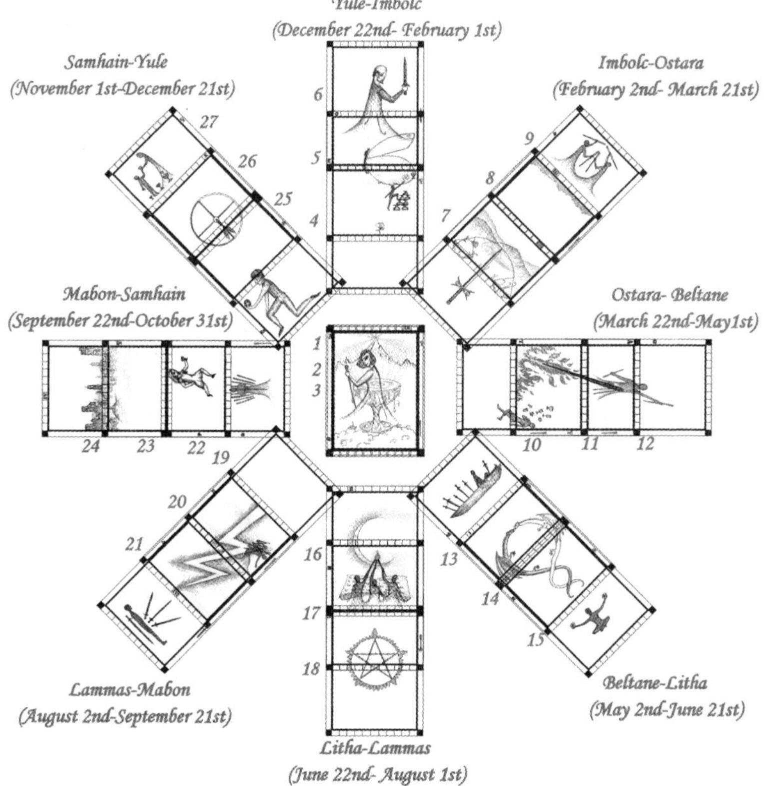

The first three cards to be placed are combined normally in the centre of the spread. These three cards may be consciously chosen or randomly selected, and represent the central figure of the issue, whether it be a character in a story, a business, or an individual. Then, starting at the top, three cards are placed in a vertical filmstrip. Starting closest to the middle, the first position indicates a motivation for action. The following card shows the action, and the third in the sequence represents the consequence. This process is continued round in a clockwise direction, until you have a layout resembling a star with eight rays, or a wheel with eight spokes, (see illustration). When all positions have been interpreted, you may wish to unlock more ideas by revolving the meaning of the positions. Thus the first card becomes the action, the second the consequence, and the third the motivation, and so on. This can also work as a divination spread, if you wish. It has enormous potential for offering fresh perspectives and ideas.

Another level of meaning may be added if you associate the shape of the spread with the ancient Celtic wheel of the year. This holds particular promise for divination, if you wish to seek guidance for the year ahead. Each spoke of the wheel may give an idea of the events or atmosphere of that eighth of the year, as divided by the festivals, (see illustration).

Infinite Possibilities . . .

There are many techniques you may wish to try with this deck, which have never been possible before with Tarot. If you are reading for a client, try asking them to choose a number of cards, and then let them play with them. See what pictures they make, offering your own insights, and seeing if they have insights of their own. It could be a useful way of helping someone to relax if they are unsure or nervous, as well as a creative way of reading. This also has scope in therapy and counseling, allowing a child or someone with limited ability to communicate their feelings to portray them in images, or accessing feelings, memories and events which may be buried in the subconscious.

Once you are comfortable with experimenting, why not let go of structure completely and let the cards go where they will, in a manic free-for-all! Get into a real conversation with your cards, opening up a two-way dialogue between you. See what happens. How might you interpret an image like the one that follows?

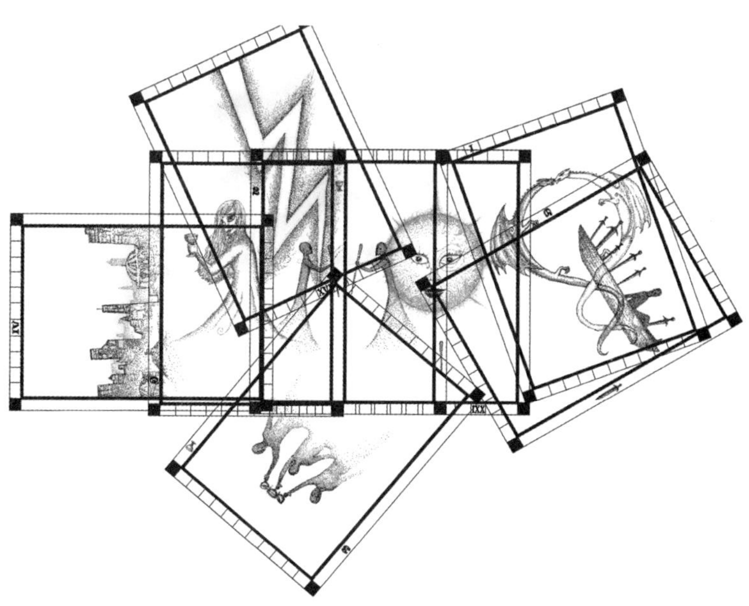

These cards can liberate you from old habits and pre-conceptions of Tarot. You could even spread out the whole deck, seeing which cards met and combined. Try choosing a number of cards and shifting their positions, combining them with each other, and see what you can learn from this process. It's a lot of fun seeing what pictures form, and you may encounter some fascinating insights into not only Tarot, but your inner self, your creative spirit and your destiny.

Good luck on your journey of discovery!

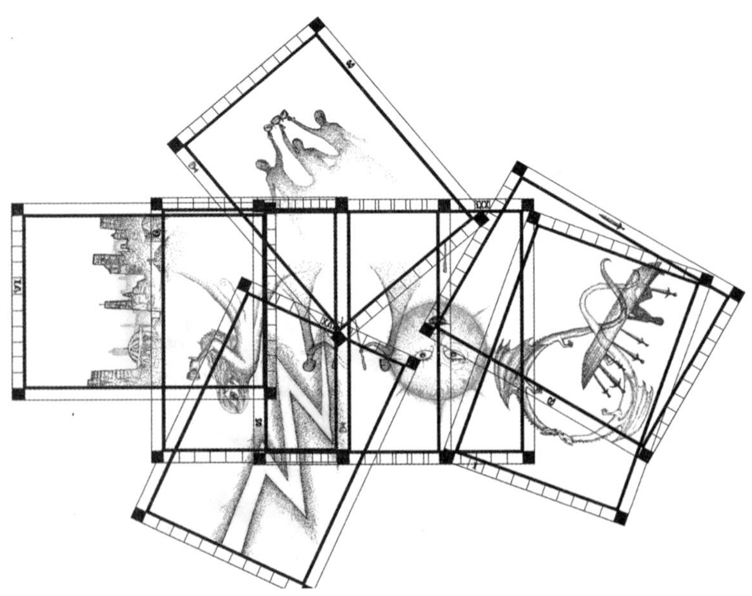